The Benjamin Franklin Lectures

of the

University of Pennsylvania

SEVENTH SERIES

The Benjamin Franklin Lectures

CHANGING PATTERNS IN AMERICAN CIVILIZATION

by Dixon Wecter, F. O. Matthiessen, Detlev W. Bronk, Brand Blanshard, and George F. Thomas
Preface by Robert E. Spiller

THE FUTURE OF DEMOCRATIC CAPITALISM

by Thurman W. Arnold, Morris L. Ernst, Adolf A. Berle, Jr., Lloyd K. Garrison, and Sir Alfred Zimmern
Introduction by S. Howard Patterson

THE ARTS IN RENEWAL

by Lewis Mumford, Peter Viereck, William Schuman, James A. Michener, and Marc Connelly
Introduction by Sculley Bradley

THE SCIENTISTS LOOK AT OUR WORLD

by W. V. Houston, W. Albert Noyes, Jr., Curt Stern, Alan Gregg, and Wendell H. Camp
Introduction by John M. Fogg, Jr.

THE CULTURAL MIGRATION

by Franz L. Neumann, Henri Peyre, Erwin Panofsky, Wolfgang Köhler, and Paul Tillich
Introduction by Rex W. Crawford

SOCIAL CONTROL IN A FREE SOCIETY

by Loren C. Eiseley, Carl G. Hempel, Gilbert Seldes, George J. Stigler, and Willard Hurst
Preface by Robert E. Spiller

TRENDS IN MODERN AMERICAN SOCIETY

TRENDS IN MODERN AMERICAN SOCIETY

by
John M. Blum, John K. Galbraith, Alexander H.
Leighton, Jonathan E. Rhoads, Eero Saarinen, David
B. Truman, Daniel D. Williams, Richard
W. B. Lewis

Edited, with a Preface, by
Clarence Morris

PHILADELPHIA
UNIVERSITY OF PENNSYLVANIA PRESS

7358

PRINTED IN THE UNITED STATES OF AMERICA

Preface

MY AIM IN WRITING THIS PREFACE IS TO STATE A VIEWPOINT FROM
which the seven papers that follow can be read comparatively. I
am emboldened to state this viewpoint because it helped me unify,
to some extent, the wide range of our lecturers' ideas; that it will
be similarly useful to others is only a hope.

Established ways are, generally speaking, the backbone of our
everyday lives. Our accustomed roles usually make one day much
like the one before it and the one after it. Of course we all suddenly shift routines when we enroll in and leave schools, when
we marry, when we change jobs, when we move to new communities, and when we are retired. Cataclysms, like wars and
economic upheavals, may push many of us out of our established
patterns at the same time. Most of us, however, live channeled
lives, by and large, with only occasional concern for the character
of the future.

When, however, we gather to hear an eminent man talk on an
important topic we are likely to expect him to play the seer. The
earlier published six volumes of Benjamin Franklin Lectures all

7

are pointed at changes in the offing. This seventh volume is cast in the same mold. Whenever our committee starts to plan a new series we seem to turn naturally to what is ahead.

Perhaps we do this because our own interests are mainly in the past, the present, and the very immediate future. Perhaps we are attracted to prophecy because it is an energizing change from our intellectual diets.

I am inclined to believe, however, that our motive in asking speakers to peer into the future is more significant; it is a reflection of the character of the Western world—especially of the character of the United States. By asking able visitors to talk about the future we make occasions for concern with the gospel of progress—with our aspirations (what they are and what they should be), with emerging opportunities for getting on, and with occasions for avoiding turns that could thwart our hopes. Nearly all of us hold (with varying degrees of conviction and articulateness) to this gospel of progress; hence our anxious concern about the future.

All nations have aspirations. But progress has been especially the hope of the West. Eastern countries are not always similarly bent: dynastic China, for example, rarely attempted progress— for two millenniums it aspired, mainly, to emulate the golden age of the reigns of the Five Ancient Emperors.

All nations have aspirations. But this does not mean that all their people aspire. Workers exhausted daily by struggles with starvation rarely have energy for aspirations that are more than vain hope. Serfs or peasants, tied to land and steeped in philosophic acceptance of flood and drought, seldom have courage enough for aspirations that are more than desire for good luck. Artisans, whose pride in craft skills (whether polishing diamonds or practicing ballet) absorbs all their existence, are too self-centered for aspirations other than complimentary notoriety. Only a community that frees its members from overwork, insecurity, and narrowness produces a society of properly aspiring men. This the West has not yet fully accomplished; but few nations have seen such melioration and hope for melioration as that which we enjoy.

Widespread participation in formulating the public's aspirations can come about only after three conditions are met. (1) Adults must, generally, have a real (not merely theoretic) right and opportunity to participate in an opinion-making that can, in turn, influence the behavior of public servants. Widespread suffrage is not enough; there must be ongoing opportunity to contribute to public opinion—a right that counts. No nation has implemented such a right; but we have no special reason for despair. (2) The definition of public servant must both broaden and become more meaningful. Power elites in business and professions must recognize that they at times deal with public, rather than private, matters. Public toleration of their power on these occasions is not oversight; it is enfranchisement coupled with responsibilities to the public rather than to shareholders, associates, and fellow professionals. Public servants (in or out of governmental office) must recognize that they are enfranchised to implement public aspirations and that whenever they act as principals (rather than as the public's agents) they act for themselves and not in execution of their trust. Even those who are utterly well-meaning in their attempts to do what is best for the public, but who act without regard for public aspirations, rule—but do not serve. (3) Technology bearing on public problems must be more widely explained and understood. The public cannot aspire to less unemployment, better mental health, sounder city planning, etc., unless it knows more about how these ends are achieved. We have learned that ends considered apart from means are likely to be futile or misunderstood; we are now learning that dissemination of knowledge about means stimulates formulation of new ends of which the uninformed would never even dream.

Still to be proved, however, is whether a pluralistic, alert, educated, and emboldened public can formulate aspirations that can, in turn, be translated into action. If a people's will is so diverse and unrestrained that it will not tolerate public servants who do anything but mark time, its aspirations become its greatest liability. Survival and enhancement of American democracy through depression and war are some bases for believing in our ability to translate a still wider public's aspirations into programs of action.

Our desire to look to the future is, of course, not limited to implementing our hopes for health, affluence, and the importance of the common man. We aspire also to more scientific knowledge, and greater beauty, more understanding of the human condition. In our Western fashion we harbor some hopes for progress in science, art, and religion.

We are not foolish enough to suppose that progress in all sciences depends on either our type of political background or our opportunities for free thought. Many sciences have flourished in the U.S.S.R. and many are likely to flourish in Red China. We have yet to see, however, great development of pure social science in these countries. If all knowledge of society must conform to the Marxist-Leninist prescription, then knowledge of society is seldom worth looking for, and may be dangerous to see. Only when stubborn facts conflict with official theory is skill brought into play, and then merely to explain a seeming contradiction. It is a good guess that progress in social science is more likely to be accomplished in the West. With that progress to build on we may be more likely than the Communists to find ways of feeding both the resulting knowledge and the fruits of physical and biological sciences into the unofficial, indeterminate processes of formulation of the aspirations of our public.

We are not so sure about the gospel of progress's application to the arts. We hold to towering beauties in our cultural heritage, sometimes without hope that they will ever be equaled, much less surpassed. But our tradition of progress makes us reject contemporary attempts of artists, writers, or composers to work in by-gone styles. In China a seventeenth-century Ming painter could be the leading landscapist of his time while trying to paint in the style of the fourteenth-century Yuan painter, who in turn avowedly had tried to produce additions to the work of an eleventh-century Sung artist. We, however, want no twentieth-century Mozarts, Shakespeares, or Michelangelos. Even when we are unhappy with modern works we nevertheless demand that contemporary artists create appropriately for our times.

In religion the place of progress is still more doubtful. To the orthodox no progress is possible, even though they live uneasily with primitivisms of doggedly unchanging human institutions. To the unreligious only disregard for (or of) religion is progress, even though they live uneasily with dampers on their own reverential twinges. If progress there is, it must lie between these two— for those who wish to search for it. It is interesting to see that so strong a supporter of orthodoxy as Jacques Maritain nevertheless can hold for progress, and assert man's increasing knowledge of natural law.

———

Those who read these papers but did not hear them delivered have missed a pleasure that we at the University of Pennsylvania enjoyed. We are grateful to the seven lecturers for their contributions.

This preface cannot be closed without acknowledging impor-

11

tant debt to Dr. William E. Miller, bibliographer of the Furness Memorial Library, who with perceptive restraint carefully prepared these papers for the printer and checked the proofs. His conscientious and skillful work is greatly appreciated by the editor of the volume and the University Lecture Committee.

Clarence Morris

Philadelphia
February, 1962

Contents

13

University Lecture Committee

13

TRENDS IN MODERN AMERICAN SOCIETY

Exegesis of the Gospel of Work:
Success and Satisfaction in
Recent American Culture

John M. Blum

MARK HANNA, ACCORDING TO A STORY AS THOMAS BEER RELATED IT, was one day reading in his suite at the Arlington Hotel. He was lost in a book, somewhere in Egypt or Assyria, when a caller entered the room. Looking up, Hanna said suddenly: "Isn't it funny, Jackling, that money and machinery came into the world at the same time?"

Perhaps Hanna had been reflecting that, since birth, neither had ever been able to leave the other long alone. Expanding through continuing interaction, they swelled the stock of goods. The diversion of a fraction of the surplus put Hanna in his comfortable suite. Had Jackling asked, the senator would probably have told him bluntly that anyone who labored hard enough could earn a likely chance for a comparable apartment. Investigation of Egyptian history, he might have added, was just digression.

Yet in the fifty years since Hanna's contemplations, machinery and money have inverted the priorities by which he lived. In the culture of today's advanced technology, Americans are increas-

17

ingly anxious about leisure, whereas less than three generations ago, with Hanna they worried more often about work. The occasions for that change are inseparable from its implications, for like money and machinery, the economy and the culture have developed in uninterrupted reciprocity. Their current forms ordinarily have puzzled Hanna's spiritual heirs.

In the United States of Hanna's childhood, there was no reasonable alternative for work. While society was passing from an agrarian through an industrial stage, hard work provided the necessities for subsistence and the surpluses for investment in further growth. Industry and frugality were essential virtues for social progress. They were concurrently sometimes the real and ordinarily the presumptive qualities for personal success and its attending social status.

That had been the case at least since the time of Benjamin Franklin and the cluster of ideas which he so self-consciously represented. His was the first great American success story, the model, one hundred per cent genuine, for latter-day heroes of myth and reality. The pattern has the soothing familiarity of legend. A poor boy, self-educated and self-made, Franklin became the first citizen of the colonies and one of the first of the western world. A shrewd statesman and able scholar, he was also a *bon vivant* who often abjured the temperance he preached and practiced abstinence only so long as he had to. Yet the self-image he constructed in his *Autobiography* accorded with those virtues he praised in his role of Poor Richard, the virtues of the cult of success.

"The way to wealth," Poor Richard instructed, ". . . is as plain as the way to market. It depends chiefly on two words, *industry* and *frugality*. . . . He that gets all he can honestly, and saves all he gets (necessary expenses excepted), will certainly become *rich*." And therefore, Franklin often implied, respected. Working and saving brought riches and riches brought status.

He was, of course, describing himself and his own formula for an incomparable social ascent, but he was also describing a dream which could in his time materialize most readily in America. He was a symbol of the possibilities inherent in an open society, a symbol dear to his countrymen. Patently Poor Richard also embodied the system of values that Weber and Tawney have called the Protestant ethic. It was a system of the first importance for the development of an economy far richer in land than in labor or capital. Work and thrift supplied the necessary compensatory force to transform the magnificence of the continent.

The transformation was not yet complete in the decades after the Civil War. The national gospel of work then received a vulgar but pervading rephrasing from Horatio Alger, Jr., who repressed a reckless hedonism only when he wrote.

Alger's message took its characteristic form in the story of "How Johnny Bought a Sewing Machine." Johnny was the son of the Widow Cooper, who had lost her husband at Fredericksburg. Though the boy wanted to go to work, she insisted he remain at school while she sewed to supplement her pension. Determined to ease her lot by buying a sewing machine, Johnny labored after school and during week ends, picking cranberries at two cents a quart, running errands, turning the grindstone. He accumulated only $50 in a year, but he persevered. One morning, crossing the fields near a small pond, he heard a gentleman in a boat call out that his daughter was drowning. Unhesitatingly Johnny plunged in and seized the child as she sank for the third time. The grateful father pressed upon the boy a $100 bill. "Now," Johnny cried, "I can buy Mother a sewing machine." Then the whole story spilled out. The girl's father arranged to purchase the machine and have it sent to Johnny's mother in time for her birthday. When it arrived, "Her eyes glistened with pride and joy as she heard, for the first time, how [Johnny] ... had worked for months." He did not know it, but the machine had cost lots more than $100. More marvelous still, he received a letter from his benefactor containing $100 for himself. "Continue to love and help your mother," it read, "and when you are old enough to go into a store I will receive you into mine." There was, Alger concluded, great joy in the little cottage that evening.

Doubtless Alger's readers felt the joy themselves, for the story was a perfect metaphor of a national faith. Johnny was a dutiful son of a fond mother who saw to his education. That showed he had the right stuff in him. Johnny had worked and saved, not in spite of adversity, but because of it. That was pluck, a folkword for character. Johnny had happened upon an accident which made his main chance. That was luck, a folk-word for a secular divinity. Johnny had won commercial opportunity, and simple projection assured him of eventual success and social position. Santayana, for many years a neighbor of aspirant Johnnies, summed up their metaphysic well: "Irreligion, dissoluteness, and pessimism—supposed naturally to go together—could never prosper; they were incompatible with efficiency. That was the supreme test." That was the exegesis of chapter and verse, James, i. 22, "Be ye doers."

Early in the twentieth century, however, the problem of sufficient production no longer existed within the United States. The nation's superb natural endowment had always contained the promise of abundance. The massive movement of peoples to the country and westward within it had provided a necessary pool of labor and a market for goods. The advantages of a free society and a vast, free market had encouraged the accumulation and investment of capital. As enterprise flourished, American business had completed the organization of conditions of plenty. The consolidation of industry made possible the efficiencies of integration and diversification, the acceleration of technology, and the professionalization of management. The twentieth century was still young when Henry Ford and Frederick Taylor, devoted disciples of the gospel of work, accomplished their prodigies of production, when during World War I the United States supplied not only its own ordinary and emergency needs but also the extraordinary demands of most of western Europe. Certainly by 1915, probably years earlier, the nation had in hand the resources and the techniques to furnish luxuries as well as necessities for a far larger population than it contained.

By that time the cult of work, thrift and success had lost some of its following. Labor was persuaded that the earth would spin just as swiftly if the work day were nearer eight than ten hours. The owners of the machines that helped to encourage that persuasion still resisted it, often with the argument that hard work never hurt anybody, but some of them were also in their own ways violating the cult. Vacations had become more common and longer. More sons and daughters of wealth were deliberately unemployed. With success, moreover, frugality frequently yielded to ostentation.

Though conditions had changed, and the culture, too, the idea of work survived the era of its basic relevance. Theodore Roosevelt, by any measure a national hero in 1903, then told one audience that work was "absolutely necessary; . . . no man can be said to live in the true sense of the word, if he does not work." At times self-consciously a Jeremiah, he attacked most viciously the idleness and folly of the rich. In a similar vein, Thorstein Veblen chose the leisure class as the particular target for his censures, reserving his fondest blessings for the "engineers," creatively productive men whose fulfillment came from work.

Roosevelt and Veblen were members of a generation that lived through the stage of mechanization which carried the United States once and for all across the brink of industrial abundance. The engineers, by the time Veblen arranged their apotheosis, had already worked their powerful magic on the price system; and the strenuous life, when Roosevelt lived it, had to spend its furious energies seeking adventures as substitutes for productive labor. Yet those who in their youth had covenanted with the gospel of work clung, not surprisingly, to their obsolescent ethic.

So strong was the national faith that it instructed at least one later generation. Twenty years after Roosevelt's most successful campaign, the chairman of the board of a large corporation employed Algerine language to explain the promotion of a company officer. "I'd put it this way," he said. "Albert Salt was the best office boy we ever had, the best clerk we ever had, the best salesman we ever had, the best purchasing agent we ever had, and he never knew when the whistle blew." Such incantations struck notes to which the middle class still responded. The popular novels and stories of the 1920's, repeating the success theme, held up to Albert Salt and his would-be companions a mirror in which they could admire themselves. The same novels suggested that indolence and elegance alike encouraged licentiousness, a disease to which artists and intellectuals, presumably marginal workers at best, were particularly subject. Greenwich Village and the Left Bank were the havens of exiles, as one of them recalled, who were fleeing the culture of their high schools, the still virulent cult of work. Even Franklin during the 1920's was rather less popular as a symbol than was Albert Salt, for unlike him, Franklin had a cultivated taste for wine and women, rest and speculation. Those diversions from productive work and careful thrift were the undoing of Sam Dodsworth. As middle class readers pitied him, so they esteemed without stint that most virtuous of American engineers, Herbert Hoover, an Albert Salt of an heroic scale.

Esteem was the ultimate article of the total faith. Work and thrift, pluck and luck brought success which earned man status. That progression was central to the creed which faced a shattering challenge during the 1920's when Americans were shown a short-cut to esteem—a short-cut, moreover, that reckoned thrift a vice. With the problem of production solved, industry's next problem was sales, and its next solution, advertising, which had to reach and stimulate the national market. In order to teach Americans to buy more than they needed, though rarely as much as their growing enterprises were producing, advertising had to disseminate an abbreviated image of the good life. It sold esteem.

Of course it also sold many other good things. Advertisements for soap sold cleanliness; for orange juice, health; for mouth wash, romantic love. But most of all advertising sold success. These clothes, that furniture, this correspondence course, those houses, and especially these automobiles were made the appurtenances of success. Ownership brought success itself, ordinarily in company with a beautiful woman, and ownership was simplified. One could buy today and pay tomorrow in regular, small installments. No need to wait, no need to save, and the interest rate, while hideous, was hidden.

As the advertising profession has so often claimed, its techniques exposed demands and did not create them. The exposure necessarily associated available and marketable commodities with more remote and sometimes impalpable aspirations. Powerful aspirations, after all, long predated the layouts that translated sex into antiperspirants, appetite into electric grills, and vigor into breakfast cereals. So, too, and emphatically, with status. If success had not already become an American fetish, advertising could scarcely have invented it. The triumph of advertising derived from divorcing esteem from sweat and denial.

Similarly advertising encouraged waste. Alfred Sloan understood the situation exactly. Just as General Wood had realized

that the drift of population to the cities would give Sears, Roe-
buck a larger stake in retail stores than in mail-order catalogues,
so Sloan realized that mechanization permitted General Motors
to manufacture cars much faster than its customers could use
them up. As one executive put it, "The old factors of wear and
tear can no longer be depended upon to create a demand."
Neither could beauty or performance alone, but advertising
could hasten obsolescence, and though some company engineers
were unhappy, G.M. made fashion the pavement of its road to
glory. As with automobiles, so with many consumer items, the
date and packaging determined the measure of esteem.

Yet here again advertising was rather more revealing than
revolutionary. Waste, as David Potter has pointed out, had always attended American experience in abundance. The nation
had condoned a profligate use of land and minerals and a reckless spoilage of timber, water, even air. Indeed a willingness to
waste may have been an indispensable part of the essential spirit
of bullish speculation that force-fed innovation and overbuilt
facilities in expectations of unending growth. These expectations
in turn supplied the means for their own ultimate satisfaction.
But if waste had long existed, and with importance, it had not
been counted a quality of success. Rascals were spendthrift, but
good men, wise and frugal, until advertising drew a beard on
savers and shaved clean the purchasers of fashion.

In attaching esteem to ownership, as it did, advertising sub-
stituted a static value for the kinetic attributes of the Alger story.
The fact of acquisition replaced the process of achievement. The
success image lost its motion. This was a portentous but possibly
essential change, for the professionalization of American life,
especially of American business, had increasingly separated the
Alger myth from reality.

Whatever the absolute values of work and thrift, they had become in themselves weaker and weaker levers for success. As the studies of William Miller demonstrate, in business as well as in law and politics, the elite of each generation since the early nineteenth century had been recruited in increasing proportion from the ranks of the children of the elite, children blessed with the advantages of economic security, higher education, and influential friends. Careers in America remained more open to talent than they did in any other society, education remained more readily available, and self-made men still received invitations to join old and exclusive clubs; but the percentage of those who were born to families of farmers or workingmen, and yet rose past the level of farmers or foremen, was diminishing continuously. This deceleration of social mobility, a function of the institutionalizing of American life, threatened to destroy the old success image and, with it, one fetching promise of the past.

By redefining the image, the hucksters distorted it, to be sure, but they also preserved it. The Alger story was among other things only one expression of a larger image of a society of opportunity, plenty, and human dignity. Madison Avenue, contriving a new recipe from old ingredients, simply associated opportunity and dignity with shared abundance. That association made the standard of living as well as the nature of work a gauge of esteem, perhaps especially of self-esteem. With high wages, a laborer, however mean his job, could be fashionable, and therefore, in his view and that of many others, successful.

Under the pressure of advertising, the conspicuous consumption and conspicuous leisure that had so worried Veblen gradually became aspirations of Americans in all walks of life. Those who so aspired, including a sizable fraction of the middle class, suffered special frustrations during the great depression. Beginning with the New Deal, however, there has been a broad redistribution of wealth, public provision of marginal economic security, and a rapid growth of labor unions. Along with these developments, the extraordinary economic recovery that the war effort spurred and the continuing prosperity of the postwar years have placed the expectations advertising nurtured within the range of probable fulfillment for the majority of an affluent society. Perhaps necessarily, ownership and fashion now weigh far more in the scales of the image of success than do industry and thrift.

Along with other twentieth-century developments, advertising affected earlier ideas about work. Artificial obsolescence was a continuing charge against the integrity of a product and consequently against the satisfactions of manufacturing it. There could be small sense of purpose in making something only to have it sold and thrown away. Doubtless mechanization itself, as Ortega observed, cost laborers much of their involvement in their jobs and perhaps all of their identification with their products. Advertising, by acclaiming waste, at the very least exaggerated the resulting loss of dignity in work. Albert Salt never knew when the whistle blew, but he was an office worker. His counterpart at a punching machine, employed in a routinized job fabricating a disposable artifact distinguished primarily by its salability, heard the whistle loud and clear. So also increasingly did office and professional workers whose own functions were made more and more mechanized, more and more specialized, more and more routine. The Algerine view of virtuous industry could not persist where labor lacked mission and work lacked joy.

Perhaps just in time, the changing culture endorsed the ready compensations of more income and more leisure, luxuries that a bountiful technology made possible. Advertising did not destroy the old cult. Rather, it expressed the values of a society in which there were no real problems of production. The culprit, if there was a culprit, goes often by the name of progress. There are still no major problems of production. The national stock of resources and skills can amply satisfy the foreseeable needs of a growing population for consumer and producer goods and for national defense. There are other problems, of course—problems of social goals and social organizations, problems of pace and allocation, problems of priorities for individuals, for neighborhoods, and for the whole nation. Many of these defy easy solution, but none can be solved primarily by more or harder work as Alger's generation thought of work. Like higher real wages, greater leisure has probably come to stay.

Indeed under contemporary conditions the old exhortations are no longer convincing. Johnny wants to buy a Chevrolet, not a sewing machine, and his mother, whose pension is now generous, approves. She is also not so sure that hard work never hurt anybody. That may have been true of picking cranberries and turning the grindstone, physical work out in the fresh air. Johnny will do well to mow the lawn. But hard work at a desk or in a laboratory or with a group of people, work involving primarily intellectual or interpersonal skills and their application, can hurt almost anyone who fails to find the time for rest and recreation. Johnny's modern benefactor is doubtless at his office every year more nearly sixteen hundred than thirty-six hundred hours, and Johnny knows it. Johnny has still the right stuff in him. He goes to school, loves his mother, heeds the example of his elders, wants to become a useful and prosperous lawyer or engineer, but he considers Alger's Johnny (if he must consider him) "out, man, way out." He has no compelling cause for thinking otherwise.

Entirely apart from its relation to success, work, of course, provided satisfaction for a fortunate few. They derived from it a sense of identification and fulfillment, a sense of self and self-expression. Such satisfaction, however, was elusive, even when goods and leisure were less plentiful than they have become. Work without dignity had little to recommend it except as a means for survival. Furthermore, identification and fulfillment escaped men from every stratum of society, including many who rose relentlessly from tier to tier.

Such men, as Ralph Waldo Emerson once suggested, wanted either an instinct for recognizing their personal genius or an opportunity for giving it release. "A man is a beggar who only lives to be useful," Emerson wrote, and beggars there had to be while the economy commanded the bulk of human energy and the culture condemned an unproductive use of time. Beggars there still are in a routinized economy where fewer and fewer jobs afford scope for self-expression. Consequently, for most of the laboring force, less work for more pay comes as an unmitigated gain.

The apparent agencies for that gain, rather than the oppressive jobs, naturally evoke the workers' loyalties. On that account the labor union receives the grateful allegiance accorded to political machines seventy years ago. Today's locals, like yesterday's precinct houses, are clubs, whose members are true to each other and to their leaders, united against their opponents, hostile or uncomprehending toward criticism. Today's union officials, like yesterday's bosses, take care of their following and also of themselves, sometimes with scant regard for means, in rare but troubling cases with small regard for law. When they are attacked, whether justly or unjustly, their constituents also feel embattled, and consequently respond like partisan fans outraged by an unfavorable call at second base, whatever the umpire's vision or wisdom. The rank and file of labor are not dishonest, but they are devoted, and they are apprehensive of change lest change reduce their share in plenty, their share in the appurtenances of success. They value the results their leaders get; they are less concerned with process.

28

That is precisely the attitude also of a host of men whose overalls have an Ivy cut—teachers not the least. They value the income from their jobs or the prestige of their professions; they are not involved in work, but in success. Their lack of satisfaction is regrettable, for it breeds unhappiness, but it is not immoral, and it is most decidedly not attributable to abundance or to advertising. It has yet to be demonstrated that comfort damages character, and it is manifest that the cult of work often honored labor less for itself than for its utility in achieving status.

There is, however, a pathos in the lives of those who seek success by sending dollars out in chase of goods. John Maynard Keynes was surely right about deficits and depressions, but a society made up of men attempting to spend their way to status is scarcely a beguiling goal for 1984. It is all too clear that the salesmen of fashion have dealt in envy, not in satisfaction. Yet only a romantic nostalgia can dignify a subsistence culture. Conformity did not develop because of abundance. Indeed, abundance threatens it, for as Martin Mayer has said, conformity is the special burden of impoverished communities where people work to exhaustion and have neither the money nor the leisure to express their tastes. In contrast, the fashions of affluence, for all their fraudulence, at least have variety and sometimes even elegance.

What those fashions lack is the capacity to provide lasting satisfaction to either their producers or their consumers. And that capacity is, among other things, an attribute of style—of an excellence of purpose, form and execution that endures while vogues decline. It is a lack of style that permits the expensive vulgarity now imitated on a wider scale than Veblen's nightmares contemplated. Here advertising, ambassador extraordinary to vogue, exemplifies the problem, for advertising rarely ministers to style. That function has no commercial basis, for by enduring, style rejects the claims of artificial obsolescence, and those who, with style, find lasting satisfactions of their own, need not indulge the whims of salesmen of esteem. Those salesmen, their clients, and the media they employ have displayed small sense of obligation to propose a separation of fashion from esteem, or of status from the image of success. Indeed probably the obligation is not theirs, for neither advertising nor its servants should be expected to renounce the profits of a gospel preached so many years. Alger, after all, did not let Johnny drown.

Style, in any event, is not susceptible to mass production. The man who recognizes it, like the man who contrives it, does so alone. It is akin to what Emerson meant by genius, the disciplined expression of a creative instinct. Only exploration of the self and of its world can disclose that kind of genius, that path to style and to satisfaction. But such exploration, which demands spare time, is not universally rewarding. For those who resist it, leisure can be frightening at worst and at best drudgery, from which one escape is pointless or compulsive work. Yet leisure, far better than toil, can help uncover genius and give it vent, can bring a man to design a style of his own.

Leisure, moreover, the most common coin of national plenty, has often been in recent years the medium of inflating opportunity. In spite of all the confusions imbedded in the culture to which Madison Avenue adheres, there is impressive quantitative evidence that Americans have seized their chance to spend their wealth for time and tools to use it. There are, most obviously, the power saws in the cellars and the dry flies on the lakes; there are the gardens, the sailboats, the skis, the bedrolls from Albany unfurled in Montana. For hundreds of the growing thousands who can acquire them, these are more than diversions, more than toys. They are instead the instruments of a process chosen to engage a legitimate pride in skill or a poignant rapport with nature. Those satisfactions are neither mean nor silly nor, in the balance, expensive. They are, in Emerson's sense of the word, the very essence of genius.

Other quantities measure different satisfactions. There are the palettes and pianos, the titles in soft covers, the records, the tents for summer symphony and theater. Never anywhere have intellectuals had larger audiences, the arts more patrons, or patrons wider choice. Leisure and abundance have set off an explosion of high culture throughout America, and hundreds of the growing thousands who paint or play or listen have found both joy and style in the processes of their minds. That represents a genuine success—a success devoid of status and achieved during a leisure curiously akin to work.

The quality as well as the quantity of goods and leisure Americans consume has been rising. Perhaps there has been no relative increase in the number of great artists. Certainly ugliness still abounds. But with abundance there has been a discernible education of taste and a mounting demand for beauty. There is evidence of these changes in architecture, city planning, and commercial design. There is also evidence in the offerings of the movies, television, and the printed media. So, for example, the incidental music of the omnipresent westerns has been acquainting children with subtle harmonies their parents rejected as discord.

Refinement, as always, has proceeded through stages, and the sophisticated, as always, have tended to deplore its pace, but pessimism need not accompany their meritorious impatience. Culture, as it were, has moved in the pattern that George Fitzhugh ascribed to labor. There has been at the bottom an unavoidable mudsill of slaves to the vulgar and the banal. Yet each cultural quake has lifted mudsill and mountain peak alike. As one American recently reminded British critics who deplore the horrid and the sham they see across the ocean, the cultural

31

tribulations of Americans are not their own alone, but the shared experience of mass society in this century. Compared to other peoples. Americans have done well. Indeed, under conditions of plenty, conspicuous emulation has proved to be an effective agency for communicating gradually the advancing standards of an intellectual elite.

A better agency of communication is education, through which leisure has scored its largest triumphs. Half a century ago illiteracy thrived on child labor. Now both are substantially erased. American children have the spare time to learn to read, though the means they employ may sometimes be inefficient, and the time to go at least through secondary school, though not all of them elect to. Most of the marginally talented can find the time and means for college, and more would do so were there available the necessary public funds and private motivations.

For all its shortcomings, the national performance in education has set significant precedents during the past fifty years. The elongation of schooling has depended upon a distribution of general wealth in the form of leisure and facilities to individuals of less than average means, including those in communities of less than average standing. Those individuals who have labored at that leisure have confirmed the promise inherent in the fading cult of work. Their productive use of time has opened to them opportunities for both kinds of success—for the careers that society esteems and, more important though less honored, for the satisfactions that trained minds achieve.

The gospel of work always made an allowance for education as a factor in the success of esteem. "Learning," Franklin said, "whether speculative or practical, is . . . the natural source of wealth and honor." Alger's Johnny's mother insisted on her son's completing school. Though it was the success of satisfaction that meant more to Emerson, education, in school or out, was in his view the dowser for the genius for which he sought release. "Half engaged in the soil, pawing to get free," he wrote a century ago, "man needs all the music that can be brought to disengage him. . . . If trade with its money; if Art with its portfolios; if Science with her telegraphs through the deeps of space and time can set his dull nerves throbbing . . . make way and sing." The kind of education he endorsed pointed that way. It exposed, thus inviting adventure, which then with experience made discipline the haversack of discovery.

Without denying education that non-directive inspiration, Alfred North Whitehead demanded for it a sharper aim. "Culture should be for action," he wrote; and formal liberal education, he believed, taught men to act, for it whetted their perceptions and instilled a sense of manner. It taught them style, in Whitehead's phrase, "the last acquirement of the educated mind, . . . also the most useful." "With style," he wrote, "you attain your end and nothing but your end. With style the effect of your activity is calculable."

Useful for men who take their satisfaction in their work, style in Whitehead's sense is no less useful for those who must seek like rewards in leisure. The very abundance of spare time invites action disciplined by education, action no less fulfilling because it is essentially private. "Style," Whitehead concluded, "is the ultimate morality of the mind." With it, a new freedom of time makes possible a new plenty, not of more goods and services, but of creative experiences that set man's dull nerves throbbing, and lift him beyond Emerson's depths of space and time.

In an age of leisure, the want of a liberal education, the absence of a morality of the mind, too frequently converts spare time to anguish, especially because society persists in unthinking incantation of the values of the cult of work. The resulting perplexities have disturbed particularly those at or near retirement.

Lacking a positive, private mission, most elder men and women have suffered from a sense of uselessness that derives from equating both use and good with work. American society has been rich enough to support advances in medicine and public health that have lengthened life expectancies, and rich enough to provide generous, almost universal pensions. American culture, however, has yet to develop a corollary gerontology. The aged especially need to understand the uses of productive leisure, and today's children will be aged very soon.

Even sooner many of them, trained to operate the complex machines, mechanical or organizational, of a sophisticated economy, will reach a ceiling of responsibility and performance beyond which lies the risk of overwhelming ennui. Such was the brief experience just fifteen years ago of most men now middle-aged—the men who mastered radar and then sat with Mister Roberts, preferring danger to another night alone. Most of them still dread to sit alone. Their peacetime radar conquered, they fly from the privacy they fear to another flickering scope or to the empty company of togetherness. There they meet their wives, resourceless fugitives from time saved by electricity and prepackaged foods. They waste their leisure as their forbears wasted abundant land and water. So also will their sons and daughters if education emphasizes trades.

An advanced technology perforce demands longer and better schooling of technicians to manipulate its engines and its laws, but a leisure culture demands much more. It needs to educate its citizens to use their time; it needs to teach them a morality of the mind, or, as aimless artisans a century ago corrupted work, and thus themselves, they will corrupt their leisure, and thus their opportunity and their society's.

So many Americans have found themselves in leisure that there is strong reason to believe that in the future, few need be lost. But education has to help much more than it yet has. It cannot wait for cultural quakes; it must precipitate them. It cannot wait for languid and complacent office holders to offer assistance for a function they do not begin to understand. It must instruct them, and their constituents.

"It is shocking," Walter Lippmann wrote not long ago, "and indeed something in the way of a disgrace, that this country, which . . . is so rich, has not had the purpose or the will . . . or a sufficiently responsible sense of the future to provide an adequate school system." It is also shocking, and equally a disgrace, that educators have so often measured their crisis in bricks and mortar and aspirant Ph.D.'s.

There is a greater urgency. There is need to demonstrate that a system productive of wealth can also produce satisfying individuality. There is need to prove that men welcome freedom from want because they value freedom to discover and to express themselves. Any rich society can, if it will, suffuse its members with fashionable goods. Any can inflate its members' traffic in purchasable esteem. Any can give them time to spare. Leisure time is susceptible to massive use in contemplation and creativity, but leisure time has yet to be directed to those ends by a gospel of confidence, a gospel as powerful and pervasive as the outmoded cult of work.

It can be. It can be if educators transfigure the gospel of work by elucidating the best meaning of success. In so doing they will propound a gospel of leisure for men to believe and to follow. Its chapters lie deep and sure within the culture. They have been for decades the core of the content and of the purpose of liberal education, of the arts and sciences and newer social sciences which society can now ill afford to deny to any boy or girl.

The message of these arts and sciences, taught with the conviction and the vigor, the duration and universality that once attended instruction in the cult of work, opens for exploration the boundless life of the mind. That is the cradle to Emerson's genius, by which each individual first finds and then differentiates himself. That is the crucible of Whitehead's style, which directs the actions of each differentiated man. Only such men are finally successful, for only they are satisfied. Only such men, in the last analysis, are free. They will not long remain so if they suffer the contemporary Algers their wasteful affluence. They have instead to teach the new, the now inclusive leisure class to work to find the private satisfactions so abundant in their plenitude of time.

The Strategy of Peaceful Competition

John K. Galbraith

ONE OF THE NEW AND COMPARATIVELY ENCOURAGING PHRASES THAT have recently come into the language of international relations has been peaceful competition. We are being told, with that impressive combination of certainty and unction that we use when we do not know, that our relations with the Soviet Union will increasingly be governed by such competition. Since, in this world, we may safely seize on any encouraging trends without being unduly encouraged, we may hope that this will be so.

In any case, this is the only kind of competition on which anyone can reflect with any comfort. And we should not be without hope. Clearly there is a growing appreciation of the new dimensions of destruction by modern weapons. That these had changed the calculus of war was urged by the well qualified after Hiroshima and Nagasaki. Perhaps so large a lesson required time to sink in. And certainly we were fortunate in having had these years during which it could penetrate the refractory materials protecting the human intelligence. For one senses that even the professionally bellicose are becoming more restrained these days. Even the professional global strategists—those whom World War II gave an exciting insight into the theory and attractively remote practice of mass destruction —have, one feels, been losing their enthusiasm for universal annihilation.

It would be wrong, surely, to imagine that this modest accretion of wisdom and caution is confined to our side of the Iron Curtain. Whatever the peculiarities of the Russian temperament or the Communist commitment to its faith, there is no reason to think that these include a predilection for high temperature incineration. This being so, perhaps we shall have an increase in peaceful caution and a diminution in bellicosity on both sides. But my purpose is not to argue for this prospect but to assume it and to examine the nature of the resulting behavior.

2

The goal of military competition is relatively simple, even though the common feature of military strategists from Darius to Hitler has been a grievous inability to make things go according to plan. The goal, if the occasion arises, is to subdue the enemy with a minimum of damage to yourself. Indeed war has become impractical because this simple goal has become impractical. With modern weapons, even given a considerable superiority, there is no way a country can minimize damage to itself—even its own weapons may, under some circumstances, do it irreparable harm. And planning is almost certainly now more subjective than ever, although the planner is protected by the unlikelihood that he will survive to learn that he was wrong.

The alternative to military competition, it is usually assumed, must be economic competition. The first having become too disagreeable, we turn to the next most unappetizing thing. As commonly envisaged, this competition amounts to a production contest. The Soviets seek to outproduce us so we must seek to outproduce them. They seek to surpass us so we must surpass ourselves. In this race, the prize is awarded to the country with the greatest annual increase in its Gross National Product.

In recent years our Gross National Product has been increasing at a rate of rather less than three per cent; the Soviet increase has been better than seven per cent. Those with a considerable sense of urgency say our immediate job is to raise our rate of growth and so to protect our considerable headstart. Those who wish to reassure us say not that we should allow the Soviets to overtake us but that their figures are wrong. A small but flourishing industry is now devoted to proving statistically that the Russians' growth isn't what it is cracked up to be. Its Mike Todd is Mr. Colin Clark, the Australian and Oxford economist, who all but establishes that Russia is going backward.

Our rate of economic growth has not been satisfactory in recent years. There has been unnecessary unemployment. Incomes of important groups have lagged. Our present machinery of public finance gets revenues for urgent public purposes with ease only out of expanding revenues. Growth settles many other problems—of this let there be no doubt.

And the Soviets are, indeed, challenging us to a production race. They proclaim their intention of overtaking us in every park and factory. One of their most successful industries must be the production of pictorial statistics for posting on walls. We certainly must assume they are serious.

But to imagine that our competition with the Soviets consists in meeting their production challenge would be a major mistake. Economic growth means one thing to the Soviets and

39

something very different to us. To a point they can win by pursuing this goal; we shall surely lose if we do so.

The U.S.S.R. was until recent times a backward and mainly agricultural country with a low standard of living. In such a country, a rapid rate of industrial growth and a rapid increase in agricultural productivity are important. They allow for an increase in present living standards and pave the path for future advance. They enable increased investment in technical and scientific advance. They provide a surplus for overseas use in support of foreign policy. It would probably be foolish in this world to imagine that military calculations will be absent from the most peaceful of peaceful competition. To a point, increased industrial capacity has a bearing on military effectiveness. However, this is a relationship that is much misunderstood and I will return to it presently.

In the U.S.S.R. there is a special need for increased production in a world where other countries have a more advanced industrial plant and a much higher standard of living. For the demonstration effect, as economists have come to call it, of wealth and well-being in other countries creates a presumption of inferiority —of being second-best. Everywhere in the world this is the effect of American living standards. It operates with special force in a socialist or Communist country, for there inferiority in living standard carries the implication of inferiority of system.

But these considerations do not hold, and certainly not with equal force, for us. The Russians want more because we have more. But we must ask ourselves *why* we want more. There must be a better reason than merely seeking to keep ahead. A mere statistical race, in which we turn in the best results for the sake of the bars on the charts, would be a futile thing. It would stir us to no enduring sense of national purpose. It would arouse no enthusiasm save among the statisticians, and no one but a statistician would be able to judge between the competing claims of the statisticians as to who had won.

When we examine the industries we would be seeking to expand with greater economic growth, we see with even more force how little there is for us in such a contest. Would we seek to increase food production? Obviously not. Surpluses are already vast. Obesity is now rather more a problem than malnutrition, and far more ingenuity now goes into the packaging of food than the producing of it. (Even here the end is in sight. The unopenable package, the goal of the container industry, is just around the corner. Thereafter the package cannot be further improved.) Similarly the need for clothing is not pressing. We now design clothes for their aesthetic or exotic, but rarely for their protective, effect. An annual automobile output of eight or ten million cars is within sight. It will bring appalling problems of storage and driving space. More of our countryside will be subject to the ghastly surgery of the superhighway. And it is a question whether the discards, wrecks, and derelicts can be recycled fast enough to prevent a hideous metallic blot from spreading out from the service stations to cover the whole land.

Some will wish to suggest that there are many individuals and families with insufficient food, poor clothing, bad housing, or who are subject to other kinds of privation. This is true. And to provide decently for these people would require more production. But first of all these people require the income or the education, health, skills and abilities which enable them to earn the income with which to buy that production. Given that income, the production that satisfies it will be forthcoming. The income or the opportunity for access to income is the place we have to start. There is no assurance merely from expanding output *per se* that the benefit will accrue to those at the bottom of the pyramid who need the goods the most.

41

It is commonly assumed that the Russians are investing in industrial plant—steel capacity, machinery and machine tools production, chemical plant—for the sake of expanding their military power. The greater such investment, the greater their power.

No one can know for sure what the Soviets have in mind. And there is also the possibility that they, like us, are guided in economic matters less by thought than by its inconvenience. What is reasonably certain is that they must be reaching the point where further increases in their industrial capacity and output add but little to their military power. In old-fashioned wars, in which steel was projected against steel, there were limits to the amount of heavy industry that could be brought into use against the enemy. In World War II, Germany, with much less steel capacity than the Soviets now have, had more than enough to equip her vast armies. With slight effort, she could have produced more steel from her available capacity; much was used for low priority purposes.[1] But modern weapons, as they are graciously called, make far less use of steel or other heavy industrial capacity than the old-fashioned kind. Also steel provides no defense against them. Unless the Soviets expect, one day, to mobilize and equip the vast armies which operated in World War II from the Baltic to the Black Sea—and believe that the plants which would do so would be allowed to operate without hindrance—then further increases in their industrial capacity can have little military relevance. A much smaller industrial plant than ours did not keep the Soviets from forging far ahead of us in the development of rockets and missiles.

If the Russians are reaching the point of diminishing returns on the military value of industrialization, then we have almost certainly passed it. Apart from its effect on public revenues, purely quantitative growth in our industrial plant adds nothing that is essential to our military strength. A much better case can be made that it weakens military capacity. Such growth provides us with goods and gadgets which we quickly come to consider necessary and which we would surrender with vast reluctance in emergency. Some of them—the automobile is a warning—may be bringing the final atrophy of our physical capacities. We are reminded of how hard it was in Korea to learn to fight an enemy that didn't ride in jeeps. Other advances —oil furnaces, motor transport, highly specialized food production—make us dependent to the death on intricate and highly vulnerable supply lines.

Finally it is said that production provides us with an exportable surplus which enables us to support our allies and to strengthen our position in the underdeveloped lands by contributing liberally to their development. But it is not a shortage of production that has been handicapping such efforts in the past. Rather it has been reluctance to employ production for these purposes—and to appropriate the necessary funds. And as this is being written, another problem is on the horizon. That is the high cost of much of our industrial output—a high cost in which an egregiously expensive steel supply plays a central role—which together with poor design is making it increasingly difficult to sell goods abroad and increasingly profitable or agreeable to supply ourselves from foreign sources. While our foreign aid and assistance help create exports, it is also the difference between large exports and more modest imports which we use to help other countries. The prices of our products—in particular the prices in heavy industry—have now become more important than their quantity. Our ability to produce a surplus for export is unimportant if it is too costly for others to buy.

So even though we may wish for a more rapid and reliable

economic growth for other reasons, a production contest with the Soviets will not much advance our cause. Without further action it would not supply the goods to the people who most need more. It would add nothing in itself to our military or economic power. And it could divert attention from more important things.

4

The objectives of the competition with the Soviets—the things which score on the board—are most vividly illuminated by the Sputniks and the lunar probes. To contemplate these for a moment is to see the true nature of the competition.

Coupled no doubt with the military threat, but by no means dependent on it, these achievements added enormously to the Soviet prestige. They modified the world-wide tendency—a tendency by no means confined to the non-Communist lands—to assume that such achievements come normally from the United States. A myth of American scientific omnipotence was dispelled. But scientific achievement has long been a source of national prestige. In Germany, France, Britain, the United States—notably also in Czarist Russia—scientific accomplishment has been a major source of national renown. In a day when science is so closely allied not only with military power but also health, physical well-being, and economic advance, it is natural that scientific prowess should be a special source of esteem. One may add that the Russians have also hit upon a form of scientific achievement with a unique capacity for advertising itself.

What the space exploration has shown is the vitality and vigor and cultural dynamism in one important dimension of Soviet society. It is this which has impressed the other people of the world, including ourselves. The Soviets have also been careful to moderate the military threat implicit in their achievement. This threat also is impressive but at the price of giving a warlike overtone to the accomplishment which detracts from the image of the boldly scientific society. The Soviets have seen that to impress, they should not unduly frighten.

If we take the Soviet success as our guide, the competition is in those things which reveal the quality and effectiveness of the social order and hence its attraction to, and repute among, the varied inhabitants of the globe. It is not a purely scientific contest. Anything which manifests the quality of the society is important in the competition so defined. Any weakness is damaging. The society with the most points of vitality and strength and the fewest of weakness will command the most respect and support. It will, one assumes, have the better chance of surviving. This, one further assumes, is the object of the race.

5

So to define matters is to see with some clarity our problems in the race and also our possible courses of action. We see again how barren the production race is—at least for us. It would add to our well-being. We should have more luxuries than before. But the rest of the world—including Russia—is already impressed by how well in general we live. Indeed we have already made too much of the American standard of living as a mark of our virtue. Consumption, conspicuous and otherwise, has always had its greatest appeal to the consumer.

We ought not assume that the competition is confined to space mechanics, as we show some signs of doing. Certainly our performance here should be far better than it has been. To the outside observer, at least, the effort seems to have consisted of a nearly unique combination of lethargy, bureaucratic rivalry, and *ex post facto* apology. We must determine to be the first to put a man in space, and it should be a public relations expert. But to confine our attention to space exploration is to limit ourselves to only one part of the competition and to a part where we are doing badly. It is, in effect, to allow the Soviets to confine the race to the things in which they have an advantage.

Above all, we must not assume that because the Soviets have a planned society and we, in general, do not, our rules preclude a planned response to Soviet initiatives. There is a dangerous tendency to imagine that faith in a free society means faith that it will accomplish everything that is needful without effort or direction. Or at most, incantation is all that is required. The effect of such a doctrine—a ruling doctrine in recent years—is to exclude an effective response to Soviet competition on grounds of principle. It means that we must fail because to succeed would be in violation of our ideology. For, in fact, most of the things which effective competition requires will also require effective government leadership. There is no alternative.

6

The indispensability of vigorous public leadership is evident when we consider the specific areas of competitive action. As noted, these consist of correcting manifest weaknesses in our social order and being aware of, and buttressing, our points of strength. Apart from the problem of race relations, of the importance of which we are on the whole aware, there are three weaknesses of our society which are gravely damaging to our reputation and prestige in the world at large and which cast a dark reflection on the quality of our society.

The first of these is the unhinged and disorderly quality of our urban society and the consequent squalor, delinquency, and crime. These are part of our world reputation for the usual reason that they are well observed by ourselves. We speak much of them and we are taken at our word. Hence the unpleasant image of violence and degradation which spreads around the world.

This is not the place for detailed diagnosis or detailed prescription, but on one thing we should be clear. This is a problem of American cities as it is not of Swedish, Dutch, German, or English cities. And it is not our problem because Americans are inherently more wicked than Swedes, Dutchmen, Germans or Englishmen. It is because we have given far less attention to the development and improvement of the urban community than have the European countries. The management of the European city is an opportunity not without its cultural and artistic responsibilities and rewards. Government in the American city remains a residual function—it does what the individual cannot do for himself, and not all of that. When a city administration is regarded as a necessary evil, we should not be surprised if it is evil.

Unemployment is the second great advertisement of inadequacy. It is especially important for it lends support to the Marxian contention that capitalism cannot function without its industrial reserve army. The traveler in the Communist lands and elsewhere finds that any explanation that he offers of unemployment in the United States is regarded as an apology—as, indeed, in some degree it is. We have developed over the years a remarkably sophisticated defense of a moderate amount of unemployment. Like the voice of a man shouting down the well, it is overpowering to the listener. But to others the beneficence of the recurrent recession is less evident. The fact that unemployment afflicts only a minority suffers somewhat from the fact that for that minority it is still a major misfortune. This is one of the instances where the man of sophistication is rendered helpless by the terrible tendency of people to remain obstinately with the unanswerable questions—in this case: Why shouldn't there be work for people who want to work?

To reconcile such opportunity with growth and reasonable stability of prices will also require public leadership.

A third weakness—actual or presumed—is the role of arms expenditures in our economic life. There is a profound conviction, perhaps only a little less deep in the United States than abroad, that our economic system is sustained only by massive outlays by the Pentagon. Remove this buttress and we would have a disastrous collapse. The point is reinforced, on occasion, by the violent movements in the stock market when there is talk of disarmament—or alternatively of heightened tension. And while the Soviets spend heavily on arms, they have managed to avoid the suspicion that this is essential to their well-being. (Perhaps it is because they have no stock market.) Those who believe that the free economy can meet and master any contingency, and that nothing helps that tendency so much as their saying so regularly, assure us (and the Russians) that a drastic reduction in arms outlays would involve no problems. The visit by Premier Khrushchev in the autumn of 1959 brought a virtual explosion of such utterances. They carried no conviction, for, unhappily, unction even when buttressed by pomposity is not a good substitute for evidence.

So our economy is thought to prosper only by the manufacture of instruments of destruction. Such an economy is unlikely to enjoy high prestige in the world; it is far more likely to repel than to attract. Yet that is our situation.

In my view we are not economically dependent on arms orders. (The politics of arms production may be more complex and serious.) Were peace to come this year or next, and were it possible to reduce our armed services to strictly ceremonial dimensions—even a ceremonial Army and Navy would now, no doubt, be very costly—we could readily replace the income so lost and the economic activity so given up. Reduced taxes on the lower income (and hence assured spending) brackets would offset a part of the loss. The backlog of public needs is massive, the equivalent, in some respects, of the accumulated personal needs after World War II. Reduction in the work week and increases in vacation time would require more workers for a given output. In particular industries and parts of the country—in the defense industries in the Los Angeles area, for example—the problem would be more serious. Part of the saving in arms outlays should be used for generous unemployment compensation for workers and severance pay for technicians, engineers and executives, and more of it might be used for grants to the cities that are specially affected. We could not make this transition without careful planning. But with planning, and aided by the accumulated consumer demand of the war years, we made a much greater transition between 1945 and 1947. Then the reduction in arms spending was from $80.5 billion to $14.7 billion. Prices were about half as high as now. So the real reduction was about three times the present total defense expenditure of approximately $46 billion.

We should map out—carefully and in detail—the course of action to be followed in the event of reduced arms spending. The existence of a clearly specified alternative to arms expenditures would show that we are not bound to this dismal industry. This would add notably to the respect and prestige accorded our economic system, both at home and abroad. It might also keep the stock market from falling when there is hopeful news on man's prospects.

7

The matters just mentioned—crime and disorder, unemployment, the seeming dependence on arms—weaken our reputation in the eyes of our own people and in the eyes of the world. They detract from the impression of quality given by our society.

Yet it would be a great mistake to think of the competition in negative terms—as purely a matter of remedying weaknesses, important as this may be. There is merit in the redeemed sinner. But the heavenly officers who pass on his redemption are men of affirmative virtue.

Without doubt the most important way of showing affirmative virtue is to have a strong and positive program of assistance to the less fortunate lands. This is not an automatic by-product of domestic economic growth and expansion; we can quite well consume all of our own output in the absence of a decision to use some of it for assistance to other people. Over the last two decades we have decided so to use some resources and we have reaped rich rewards from this decision. Critics of foreign aid might imagine what our present position in the world would be if we had been content since World War II to invest in our own comfort and well-being and let the rest of the world go by. One of the things now reasonably well established in international relations is the obligation of the richer countries to help the less fortunate lands. Historians will give us credit for this.

But in failing to see foreign aid as a manifestation of the quality of the society—as an index of its generosity and compassion and hence of its right to respect—we have severely damaged its usefulness. Ignorant and shortsighted men have regularly insisted on presenting it as a purely selfish thing. "I had one guiding principle in my conduct of ICA affairs," John B. Hollister, a former foreign aid administrator, said not long after leaving office. "Each proposed project had to be tested by a single standard: 'Will the spending of money for this purpose increase the security of the United States?' . . . my sole concern was and is the self-interest of this nation."[2]

This is slander. We have provided foreign aid mostly because we felt it was generous and right and perhaps a little out of a sense of guilt that we should be so well off while others were not. By such proclamations, we tell those who receive our help that they must consider themselves pawns in our game. No man wishes to be a pawn. The total consequence is gravely to impair the usefulness of the aid in the competition it is assumed to advance.

If we see the aid as a manifestation of the quality of our society, we will also see that it does not advertise an expedient or parochial attachment to the goals of the good society. This happens when we extend assistance to corrupt tyrannies or reactionary ruling oligarchies which are a principal menace to their own people. This also is regularly defended as the strategic course by the tough-minded and hard-headed men. We have seen recently in Venezuela and Cuba—as we shall see one of these days in the Dominican Republic—how deep is the mistrust and how great the later difficulty from such a course. Nor are the consequences confined to the countries in question. When we support tyrants and rascals, we everywhere support the impression that we are indifferent to liberty, decency, and social justice. This also we must not do. The proper and the practical courses coincide.

8

Were the Soviets to press far ahead of us in some important field of medicine or agricultural science—even in automobile propulsion—there would be more of the soul-searching to which we are becoming so accustomed. That is because we do not appreciate our advantages—and the prestige that resides therein—until they are threatened. Where there is no immediate challenge, we are inclined to imagine that there is no competition.

The lesson would seem to be reasonably clear. In science we should give at least equal attention to those fields where we are ahead and those where we are behind. Perhaps we should have some sort of regular scientific inventory to ascertain where—though ahead—we are slipping. As things now stand, or so it appears, we become aware of inadequate progress only when it puts us in second place.

But the problem of protecting and also using our advantage is not alone and perhaps not peculiarly confined to science. The scientific virtuosity of a society is only one measure of its quality. Other forms of intellectual and artistic achievement are also important. And they derive even more importance from the fact that it is the intellectuals and the artists who have both the first words and the last on the quality of a culture.

We should not be too superior about modern Soviet culture. The cultural life of the great Soviet cities is intense, professional, and interesting. Music, classical ballet, and the traditional stage are all excellent and enthusiastically supported. If some great novels get suppressed, some rather good ones now get published.

The universities are large, well attended, and well equipped. The intellectual is a person of prestige. Yet in this part of life—especially in writing, the modern theater, painting, and architecture—our lead over the Soviets is great. And our advantage lies not in superior aptitude but in superior social context. The arts, to state a proposition of no breathtaking novelty, do not flourish where they are inhibited by formal dogma.

The world accords New York the honor and prestige of regarding it as a world capital, not because of the quality of our soldiers or our scientists or our statesmen, but because of the quality of our actors, playwrights, composers, artists, and architects. (The banality of Soviet painting and architecture is one of the most damaging advertisements of Soviet society.) The Soviet universities are large but they are far less varied and interesting than ours. It is with the better of ours, as with Oxford, Cambridge, and the University of Paris, that the intellectual community of the world tends to identify itself. This is no small advantage.

Yet it is an advantage that, on the whole, we ignore. When Premier Khrushchev visited the United States, he was shown a great many politicians, including some who do not especially commend themselves to the American people and a few who bear the concise designation of crummy. He saw some distinguished entrepreneurs and quite a few who are merely impressive. He saw shrunken ornamental shrubs at Beltsville and big corn in Iowa. He also saw Perle Mesta's machine shop. All of these exhibits, apart perhaps from the politicians, may have been marginally more remarkable than anything he could have seen in Russia. But the difference is only one of degree.

By contrast, he met no writers or artists. He did not see the Museum of Modern Art or the Whitney Museum—or even the new Guggenheim Museum. His glimpse of our contemporary architecture was incidental. He missed Tennessee Williams, Arthur Miller, and Rodgers and Hammerstein. He saw no great libraries. He saw little of our universities and nothing of their members. Perhaps Mr. Khrushchev wasn't interested. And perhaps in this instance nothing could be done. But the omissions are symbolic. It is by these things, far more than by our technical virtuosity, that we earn the respect and affection of the world —including, as the visitor there discovers, that of an astonishing number of Russians.

9

I would not wish to suggest that our competition with the Soviets is in any way frivolous or soft—it may be a measure of our miscalculation on cultural matters that it is necessary to say that competition in this sphere is not. But given our genius for self-interest both enlightened and otherwise, we must be on guard against proposals put forward in the name of competition by those who would find them convenient. During Mr. Khrushchev's visit, a large advertising agency took space in the New York papers to claim that more and better advertising was our secret weapon. In the months and years ahead, we will certainly be told that our superiority turns on better filter tips, the preservation of highway billboards, resistance to pay television, and the consumption of more aged whiskey. We should treat this idiocy with the contempt that it deserves.

But in a competition to develop and reveal the quality of our society, we must not rely on the wisdom of the solemn men. They will tell us that this is no time for reform—that, as always, other things are more urgent. They will do the Russians the honor of assuming that the only form of intellectual competition is in space exploration where the Russians are ahead. They will fail to see that our greatest achievements are those that depend on our capacity for economic and social experiment and change, and on the diversity and freedom of our culture.

Finally they will hope that the bill for doing what we must can somehow be avoided. Let there be no mistake. Most of the things we must do to reveal the quality of our society will cost money—public money. Willingness both to advocate and to pay is the test of whether a man is serious. If we haven't yet learned to mistrust, indeed to ignore, the man who talks about high national purposes and then omits all mention of the price—or perhaps urges strict economy in public outlays as one of his higher purposes—our case could be pretty bad.

Notes

1. Burton H. Klein. *Germany's Economic Preparation for War.* Cambridge: Harvard University Press, 1959. See especially pp. 130 et seq.
2. *Saturday Evening Post,* March 28, 1959.

Culture and Mental Health

*Alexander H. Leighton**

THE OVERWHELMING THING ABOUT CULTURE EVERYWHERE IS ITS
state of change. We are apt to recognize this readily enough in
cultures not our own, especially in those countries called underdeveloped, but we ourselves are hardly less caught up in transition. Change is like a windstorm, gathering through recent centuries until now we are rushed along in velocity, feeling disorder
and wondering whither.

There are many reasons for alarm in this, and the possible
effect on mental health is one of them. The first question, without doubt, is survival, but the second is survival for what? Looking ahead over the next ten years I could easily predict increases
in mental illness, cast one way or another within the framework
of the world's groaning problems. I could also point out that the
deterioration of mental health is an increment to a downward
spiral: the greater the prevalence of psychiatric disorder, the less
the ability of society to cope with its problems, and the less it
copes, the greater the disorder, and so on.

But global gloom is a prejudiced view. While the times are
risky, they are also alive with opportunity and can be met with
zest and confidence that ultimate gain is worth the risk.

* Grateful acknowledgement is made to Mrs. Donna Regenstreif
for her help in collecting information pertinent to this chapter.

What actually happens with regard to mental health and mental illness in the sixties will depend on some of the events and trends now evident. These originate in part within the discipline of psychiatry itself, in part from the wider field of medicine to which psychiatry is attached, and in part from the swirling sociocultural matrix in which both are set. Although we are now blind as to how the trends will fuse, neutralize and conflict with each other, and the shape of the results in human way of life, it is possible to suggest directions and a few of the problems that will demand understanding and statesmanship.

Research on genetic factors is growing. For many years investigation of family tendencies has been in progress with the accumulation of enormous bodies of data, particularly in Scandinavia; and in this country some of the most interesting work has been based on the study of twins. To these long-established approaches are now added some that are new. The most startling is the discovery of a quick and effective technique for determining chromosome numbers and patterns in living people. This has shown, to take one example, that there are both an extra chromosome and a distortion of pattern in the cells of persons who suffer from the "Mongolian" type of mental deficiency. It is also leading to greater understanding of the constitutional aspects of sex, particularly as to degrees of difference in maleness and femaleness and to mixtures of both in one individual. Even biochemistry has been brought in. Linus Pauling has focused on phenylpyruvic oligophrenia, an hereditary form of mental deficiency, with the idea that an abnormal molecule is taking the place of a normal enzyme concerned in the oxidation of the amino acid, phenylalanine. Discoveries of this sort, while they may begin with an unusual disorder, often help uncover processes that are pertinent to many other types of illness.

The eventual promise in all this is for increased control over disease, but it brings uneasy questions. It would be agreeable to think that one day anyone born with a defect could have a compensating enzyme source implanted in his body; and to some extent this may turn out just so. On the other hand, knowledge of genetic and constitutional factors—as for instance the ability to predict with reasonable accuracy that defective children will result from the union of such and such individuals—is bound to confront us with additional problems of freedom and responsibility. Can human breeding remain couched in a philosophy of free individual choice, or must society for the sake of humanity encroach with requirements and limitations? Whatever the answer, we can expect an impulse toward re-examination of many values characteristic of our culture. If over-population is one of the world's most important and difficult problems, these advances in knowledge add a dimension that takes nothing from the importance or the difficulty, but they may increase the potentiality for health and happiness.

The discovery, furthermore, of correctives that are successful if applied early in life bears directly on the rights of parents. This is an old issue, particularly in some religious groups whose beliefs dictate the withholding of vaccination, transfusion and medication. But with every step that medical sciences make toward greater power to prevent and stop, the greater becomes the question of society's responsibility for protecting its children regardless of the cultural or sub-cultural sentiment-systems to which the parents subscribe.

Other types of organic studies suggest additional trends. One of these is toward identifying the physiological transactions which accompany certain emotional states. The history of psychiatry is littered with the dead careers of people who have tried to find a particular organic fault as *the* key to mental and emotional illness. Yet, an occasional rich strike as in the discovery of spirochaetes in the brains of paretics, together with a deeply ingrained monocausal philosophy has served to keep the effort going. This can be said even though the general trend in American psychiatry over the last 50 years has been toward psychological rather than physiological systems of explanation. One hindrance to progress has been a lack of sufficient development in the basic fields upon which discovery along these lines would depend: neurophysiology, endocrinology, and biochemistry.

Although there is no clear light yet, there is accumulation of knowledge and technical tools on a number of relevant fronts. We have known for some years now that something is loosed in the blood of a man or a woman suffering anxiety which can be detected through biological means. If some of this blood, for instance, is allowed contact with a preparation of muscle from a rabbit's intestine, the latter is thrown into spasms of contraction. Blood from a person who is not emotionally or physically disturbed fails to have this effect. The substance has so far escaped every effort to grasp and pry it open to learn its chemical nature, but methods developed and perfected in various corners of physiology and biochemistry are being applied to solving the problem. It can be expected that studies of acetylcholine metabolism, or the functioning of the thyroid will produce before long evidence of organic concomitants to some of the disturbed patterns of behavior and feeling that come under psychiatric attention. These organic changes may not turn out to be causal in any simple way, or to be independent of psychological experience. Yet, knowledge of the physiological and eventually biochemical aspects of the processes may increase the opportunity for intervention with biochemical as well as psychological correctives.

Experiments are being made with an increasing variety of drugs that produce states of mind and feeling resembling some found in mental disorder. "L.S.D." (lysergic acid diethylamide) is one well known example. Through the use of these substances with volunteers and with animals, another triangulation may be achieved on those sources of behavior which are not under conscious control. Studies of sleep and especially sleep deprivation promise advance in understanding some roots of delusions and hallucinations. Successes that have been achieved in brainwashing force attention in this direction.

A third major discovery, and one which is notable for its sudden appearance and enormous impact, is the tranquilizers. Every year this family of carbon rings and chains, which have the power to change your feelings and mind, are multiplying and giving rise to variant forms, like some new virus sweeping the world. There can be no question that they have brought vast benefit to the psychiatrically ill. In addition to reducing suffering directly, they have augmented other forms of therapy, have kept people at work and living at home who would otherwise have required hospitalization, have rendered hospital stays shorter, and have improved the atmosphere within hospitals and extended their treatment resources.

It must be recognized, nonetheless, that all of these advances which bring increased power to manipulate emotions and to influence motivation drive us deeper into problems we already have but do not yet know how to handle. One facet of this is the role of the psychiatrist as the one centrally responsible for all forms of mental healing. That the tranquilizers are being given out by all kinds of practitioners to all kinds of people, is clear enough. It is also evident that this situation is fraught with the possibility of serious consequences from misuse. The demand for relief, however, far outruns the number of psychiatrists available to mediate it. The direction in which one has to look, therefore, is toward appropriate psychiatric training for the various medical practitioners and a greater emphasis on the psychiatrist as a consultant and advisor to them.

One of the notorious things about most of the prevailing forms of psychotherapy is the length of time required. There are very great pressures to reduce this obstacle and a somewhat uncritical faith among laity and doctors alike that this will ultimately be achieved through a pill. Psychotherapists may consider this view naïve and superficial, but they cannot afford to discount the likelihood that ever more effective organic means of symptom relief will be found. If this turns out to be so, it is almost certain that the position of the psychiatrist within the medical profession will be greatly altered. The specialist in long-term depth psychotherapy may find himself in a position something like that of the chest surgeon after the advent of isoniazid and the other modern anti-tuberculosis drugs. The psychotherapist may protest that he is not technologically obsolete because the drugs are only masking unresolved psychopathology, that they should be used as an aid to psychotherapy, not instead of it, but if the drugs do provide effective relief at a cost much lower than psychotherapy, he may not find many people who will pay attention to him.

I do not mean that psychiatry itself will become obsolete, but rather to suggest that there are events which for better or worse will profoundly affect the character of what it is and does. This is a matter of concern to the psychiatrist, to medicine in general and to the people whom medicine serves. It seems probable that the drugs, as they become more effective and safe, will slip more rather than less beyond the control, not only of the psychiatrist, but of the medical profession as a whole. While the profession may for a time be successful in combatting such a trend, in the long run there is likely to be considerable revision of values, standards and practices pertaining to doctor, patient, and non-patient.

Beyond the question of realignment in the health services, the development of organic control over psychological processes must confront us ever more pointedly with a number of broader cultural issues. At the very least some of the fundamentals of our Judeo-Christian systems (embodying the Greco-Roman) shall come up for re-interpretation and some new thinking with regard to free will and responsibility. If we accept the fact that there are states of depression and anxiety beyond the power of voluntary control which are so compellingly maladaptive as to constitute illness by anybody's standards, there is just as certainly a gradation from these to the conditions of everyday living and the emotional problems which are the task of every man and woman. What shall these organic discoveries mean for conceptions of character and self-discipline, for the proper handling, or avoidance, of guilt?

Are we to believe that under certain conditions it is proper for the psyche to suffer? This is commonly assumed now, although there is little consensus as to definition of the conditions. Chemical control over the emotions will not in itself clarify the principles of responsibility, but it will heighten the need for such clarification. Are we to evolve new codes which will hold people responsible merely for taking the proper pills? Or, to look at a different side, what are to be the ethics of consuming drugs to promote fiercer competition in business and the professions? We have standards for this kind of thing in horse races; are these to be applied in other aspects of life?

There also loom closer and larger problems concerning the right of any individual or group to induce a person to take such drugs either by force or by stealth. Should parents be free to alter the personality of a child, and if so, under what circumstances and within what limits? What kind of offense will it be to give drugs surreptitiously to another which may not directly harm him, but which do affect his disposition and his decisions?

Should these drugs have a place in the maintenance of industrial or military morale for the sake of national defense? Or, in the murky areas of psychological warfare, espionage and counter-espionage?

Turning now from the organic to the psychological level in psychiatry, it may be observed again that such has been a major preoccupation in the present century, especially in the United States. Theory has grown enormously, and the importance of this should not be underrated. It must be admitted, however, that the translation of these theories into hypotheses for experiment has so far proven difficult. Even effectiveness of treatment and the relative value of different approaches are not above question, and much has to be accepted on faith. One may say, therefore, that the main trends are already manifest in such matters as interest in unconscious motivation and the dynamic character of personality development. The main contributions ahead lie in the modification of theories through testing so that some become more established and specific, while others are winnowed away.

Experimental work in animal behavior contains a forefront now so far as mental health and mental illness are concerned that has to do with conditioning and related phenomena, particularly the "imprinting" of the young so that their adult behavior is distorted. Also of note are studies into the effects of different kinds of social position on the animal's emotional, mental and physiological capacities. Some of this work shows marked disability, and even failure of individuals to survive, as a result of particular kinds of social systems. Out of such investigations there may ultimately come firm knowledge regarding the origins and nature of the ties that bind and divide human beings, rendering some people contributive, some unadjustable and some hostile to their fellows and to the business of living. If so, the knowledge will raise questions of obligation in family management and about the current ways for handling those who commit crime. Here as well as in much of what has been said in previous pages, mental health and the health of society are so interdependent as to appear often different aspects of the same phenomenon.

I come now to the final and main area selected for mention in this chapter—social psychiatry. Two activities under this heading, *environmental treatment* and *epidemiology,* have particular implications for development in the '60's and hence will be discussed at some length.

Environmental treatment in its broadest sense encompasses all that is done for a psychiatric patient aside from medication and the person to person transactions with a psychiatrist. There is currently a revolution going on in mental hospitals with emphasis on improving the therapeutic environment, and on removing harmful aspects often characteristic of large institutions. This is sometimes labeled the "open door" policy. Fundamentally, it means a more fluid arrangement between mental hospital and community and greater emphasis on running the institutions for the patients' benefit rather than the convenience of society. The move is toward admission on the same basis as to any other hospital, and similar arrangements for leaving. During hospital stay the treatment embodies practical evidence to the patient of confidence in him, with a view to mobilizing otherwise atrophied resources for self-responsibility and recovery.

This trend is creating demands for community action and services which hardly exist, or do not exist at all. Although many patients after leaving hospital maintain a productive life as members of the community, a large proportion still need some place to go as out-patients, and often some sort of visiting care at home. In many instances there is no suitable home, so that hostels or boarding-out arrangements have to be organized. Expanded programs of group psychotherapy are also desirable. Altogether, there is a demand for increased psychiatric services as such, and a demand for an increase in relevant services from the general health, education, welfare, and employment agencies.

To some extent the "open door" and much that it implies have been a component of psychiatry for a very long time. Boarding-out and community participation have been the feature of treatment at the village of Gheel in Belgium from the Middle Ages, while in the 19th century numerous variations on this theme were created in other countries, starting with Germany. The important thing to note, however, is that the success of all such efforts in community psychiatry depends as much on the sociocultural patterns of the community as on professional ideas regarding what is desirable for treating ill people.

The past flow and then ebb of earnestness, extensiveness and success with environmental treatment have been primarily due to the prevailing and then changing qualities of the surrounding culture. Nowhere is this more pointedly evident than in Germany, which bracketed the socially oriented humanity of Wahrendorff and the killing of mentally ill people under the Nazis. Lasting achievement in the present "open door" development is, therefore, dependent on the climate of values, opinion and action prevailing in our society. For this there has to be education that is both widely spread and convincing. And to be convincing it has to be congruent with other major issues and demands in modern living.

Looking beyond the present trends of environmental treatment in North America, there are reasons to suppose that within the '60's there will be stimulus for more revolutionary effort. I have in mind here some of the programs in underdeveloped but rapidly developing countries. Where we are hampered, often severely, by having first to tear down institutional structures and customary ways of doing things in order to build, those who must begin by laying the very foundations have in some respects better opportunity to be creative and effective. Some profit can be drawn by them from the errors as well as the successes of Europe and North America, and with the inspiration of their own cultural differences they may be able to try out departures.

I should like to mention impressions gained from visiting in 1959 two psychiatric enterprises in Africa, one in Sudan and one in Nigeria. The Sudanese endeavor consists in the Clinic for Nervous Disorders at Khartoum North. Founded originally in 1952 by Dr. Tigani El Mahi, it is currently under the directorship of his former assistant, Dr. T. A. Baasher. Both Tigani and Baasher are graduates of the Khartoum Medical School, were formerly public health officers, and then were qualified as psychiatrists at the Maudsley Hospital in London.

The Sudan is an exceedingly diverse land geographically and culturally. With 967,500 square miles it is three times the size of Texas, encompassing vast hot desert, steaming jungle and mountains that reach up to the snow. The total number of people is uncertain, but probably close to 11 million, of such different cultural and physical types as Nubian, nomadic Arab and Nilotic Negro. There is also variation in religion, including Coptic Christians, Moslems and Animists; and it is in the religious nexus that there takes place the greatest part of whatever mental healing is done.

Psychiatrists initiating their work in this setting have to take a look, obviously, at what is already going on. One description by Baasher of faith healing at a Moslem shrine may serve as illustration.

The place in question is in Kordofan province, in a glen with a clear flowing stream, green leaves, and mountains rising on each side. There are four "tombs" in the glen, but they do not contain the bodies of the men they memorialize. One moreover, is to a man who never actually existed, but who appeared in a dream asking to be given food and shelter. The "tomb" that is the main focus of the shrine bears the name of El Alim Taba, a religious leader who had a great following in this area many years ago.

Baasher was told that 200 visitors a day were usual, and that on some days the total rose to 500. As he went among them talking and listening he estimated that 45% were psychiatric cases, 30% were neurological and 25% were a miscellaneous group including cases of blindness, deafness and other chronic organic disorders. He saw new arrivals coming by car, donkey and camel and noted that nearly all appeared full of excited hope, in a suggestible and receptive mood. Expressions of desire and confident expectation were exchanged. Some people went around the place gently touching the walls or bending down to take a handful of the holy sand and rub it enthusiastically over their bodies. Occasionally one or more would raise their hands calling on the holy men for health and cure.

In due course, the people as a group were admitted to the precincts of the shrine and this brought a renewal among patients and relatives alike of praying, calling on the holy men for help and confirming each other's confidence. There followed then a period of waiting, males and females sitting separately. Symptoms and complaints were discussed and also the wonderful feelings they were now having. Despite tribal differences and the severity of some of the diseases, there was much exchange and building of interpersonal relationships and the growth of an atmosphere of group sympathy.

When the priest arrived, silence fell. Two assistants brought him water from the tomb where it had been kept to acquire holiness. He then stood and looked searchingly among the crowd. At length he selected an 18-year old girl displaying bizarre body movements. She was made to sit in front of the holy man, who poured the water on her forehead and into her mouth. At the end he passed his hand over her head and assured her of cure and happiness. All were given this assurance of complete and unqualified cure, regardless of their condition—whether neurosis, schizophrenia, or blindness.

So far as mental healing is concerned, Baasher drew the conclusion that some conditions might be helped, but that for many the result would be disappointment and further misery. The important thing to him, however, was the way people looked at illness, their influence on each other during the shrine visit and their capacity for being moved psychologically.

Let us turn back now to the clinic at Khartoum North. A unit within the Ministry of Health, it gives free service, is open six days a week and sees 30 to 40 patients a day. The staff, in addition to Baasher, consisted at the time of my visit in another physician training to be a psychiatrist, three medical assistants who were specialists in psychiatry, four other medical assistants in training, two female nurses, clerical and maintenance staff and a chauffeur.

The medical assistant, it should be explained, has a professional role midway between nurse and doctor. With more training than a nurse he has been developed to run general medical clinics in out-lying areas, and he assumes considerable responsibility for treatment. The further training as a specialist in psychiatry is something new.

The patient load and the resources of the clinic do not permit very much prolonged psychotherapy. Even if such treatment were possible, the cultural orientation of most patients would make it difficult or impossible for them to understand and participate in this form of treatment. It is to be anticipated, therefore, that the Clinic depends largely on tranquilizers and other drugs, on electro-shock, counselling, suggestion and direct advice. Beyond this, however, Tigani and Baasher have developed their own form of group treatment which knits together all these other methods.

Theirs is group treatment in a double sense: the patients as a group are treated by the Clinic team as a group. The patients are usually accompanied by family members, perhaps a daughter with father, mother and maybe grandparents, a young man and his uncle, or a wife with her husband and mother. After first arriving all spend some time in the waiting room and Clinic porch talking to each other of complaints, symptoms and expectations. The medical assistants move among them, engaging them in conversation. Where there are new cases, the assistants secure the main facts of medical and psychiatric history, and for old cases, what has happened since the last visit. All such information is then reported to the psychiatrist.

During the waiting and information-giving period, an atmosphere of expecting that the treatment will be successful arises. This is partly spontaneous in the exchanges between the people sitting about, both patients and non-patients. It is fostered, however, by attitudes and words of sympathy and assurance on the part of the medical assistants. It seemed to me from what I could gather through translation and from observation, that sentiments of optimism and confidence were set in motion, circulating through the group and gathering strength with each circuit.

The psychiatrist sees the patient in his office together with the accompanying family members. Following this he interviews the patient and his relatives separately. Finally the patient and his family are brought together again in the presence of the psychiatrist and the illness and treatment are discussed. One or two of the medical assistants are also on hand to participate in the discussion. Thus even here the interaction is between persons in a group and not the private doctor-patient dyad that is so basic a unit in Western medicine. The only procedure I had observed previously which approached that of this Clinic was the diagnostic and therapeutic demonstration for medical students and interns which is commonly employed in medical teaching. In these, some therapists do attempt to use exchanges with the audience for the patient's benefit, particularly as a means of suggestion, education and persuasion. Even here, however, family members are almost always firmly excluded.

At the Khartoum North Clinic the psychiatrist, already briefed by the medical assistant, conducts his examination of the patient in this group situation and draws on the others present for additional information as this may be needed. It is obvious that for better or worse he must think quickly, for within a matter of minutes he has to make his preliminary diagnosis and begin treatment through remarks directed at both patient and relatives. All, including the medical assistants, hear what he says about next steps and about the longer range therapeutic plan. No promises are made, as a rule, yet the atmosphere of kindness and assurance that things can be improved seems very strong. If the decision is for some form of physiological treatment—vitamins, sedatives, tranquilizers, electro-shock, etc.—the patient is taken aside for this, with family members still in attendance, helping to hold him in the case of electro-shock. Afterward there is another period of soaking in the atmosphere of the waiting room and porch, and then a further interview with the psychiatrist during which the therapeutic problem and requirement are further explained to both patient and relatives.

Baasher holds that for the cultural groups who come to his clinic, especially those from rural areas, this family centered treatment is far more effective than the private interview. This is because the patient, much more than in England or America, is an element in a tightly woven unit. Whatever is said or interpreted with regard to motives, emotions and interpersonal relations has to be said to all. Thus, the family is fundamentally the target of treatment and the patient's opportunity to change for the better is to a large extent determined by the creation of more healthy expectations and realignment of interpersonal relations within the unit. Baasher says he realizes that the group situation prevents many things being mentioned which might be said privately. On the other hand he feels the psychiatrist can see things in the interactions of the people before him that he would never be told.

A second point made by Baasher is that the first interview, indeed the first few minutes of the first interview, are critical in certain disorders for therapeutic success.

It seemed to me that the Khartoum North Clinic leaned excessively on suggestion and I asked if the symptom relief obtained by these methods was enduring. He said that he thought it was, but that his only basis for this conclusion was clinical impression. He then asked me if our views about the effectiveness of the treatment we use were based on better evidence.

There is much more to the Clinic than has been described in these few pages, and Baasher had many interesting ideas on psychological theory that have sprung from his efforts to adapt Western psychiatry to this complex of cultures. One such idea formulates the problem as that of helping the patient to break out of a sick role in which he has become stuck fast and to reestablish a new role within the family nucleus. Enough, however, has probably been said to illustrate the kind of point it is desired to make. As can be seen, procedures are under way that constitute innovations far more radical than anything we are likely to attempt here. They deserve to be carefully assessed for effectiveness and for implication with regard to basic theory. If it turns out they are successful both in therapeutic result and ability to handle large numbers of patients per unit of psychiatric manpower, then it may be that they can be extended to other countries with similar cultural groups.

Further than this, however, is the possibility of having them extended back to us in the West. One could not, of course, think of the Khartoum North Clinic being set up just as it is in Scarsdale, Queens or the Bowery. There may, however, be a place for an adaptation of its form of group treatment and for the use of something like its type of therapeutic assistant to the psychiatrist. Whether or not this turns out to be so, it is probable that as innovations like this arise in different parts of the world, they will have an impact on our thinking and stretch our minds to new possibilities.

The psychiatric enterprise in Nigeria is in many ways very different from that in the Sudan. Instead of a clinic, there is here a hospital for nervous diseases distributed over a square mile of grounds. Instead of desert the surrounding country is tropical savannah and tropical jungle, occupied almost entirely by one tribe, the Yoruba, numbering altogether some 5 million, mostly engaged in farming.

Nigeria as a whole extends for 338,593 square miles and has close to 40 million in population, the largest Negro country in the world, containing almost half the people in West Africa. Among these are many tribes, languages, and religions, and geographic variation from coastal swamps and bayous in the south to desert in the north. Despite its ferocious history of slaving and human sacrifices, its still spooky jungle villages and blood-soaked altars, the nation heaves with energy and zest for development, and has numerous able leaders.

The hospital in question, Aro, founded in 1954, is located outside the city of Abeokuta, about 65 miles north of Lagos. It is under the direction of Dr. T. A. Lambo, who like his colleagues in Sudan was trained at the Maudsley Hospital in London. When he took charge of Aro in 1954, Lambo had seen Tigani's work at Khartoum and he approached his task full of concern as to how to make limited personnel stretch the services provided as far as possible. At the time he was the only psychiatrist in Nigeria.

Although the hospital is modern and designed to operate according to standards accepted in Europe and North America, Lambo had misgivings from the start as to these being adequate for most Nigerians. Admittance to the hospital, for one thing, meant family separation, and many patients and families refused the services under such conditions. Besides this, the hospital was under-staffed due to lack of trained psychiatric nurses and other personnel.

There was also the factor of expense. When the hospital had its full complement, each patient would be a considerable cost to the government, his family or both, and Lambo could not foresee the day when it would be economically feasible to have enough such hospitals to meet the psychiatric needs of Nigeria.

The situation called for extemporization, and in this context he developed a combination of day hospital and boarding-out arrangement in near-by villages. At the beginning the village people were averse to mental patients living among them, but after being persuaded to try it on a small scale, the idea took hold and at the time of my visit in 1959, there were some 70 patients distributed in three villages. The basic idea is that the patient should remain as much as possible in his normal cultural setting while under treatment. This prevents withdrawal into himself and atrophy of his resources, keeps him in touch with the motions of normal living, and avoids putting him under the added psychological strain of family separation and adjustment to an utterly foreign style of daily routine.

The typical arrangement is that the patient's family rents a room in the village for seven and six-pence to fifteen shillings per month, depending on size and quality. One or more members of the family live with him and give whatever care is needed, including the preparation of his meals. To the extent his condition permits, especially as recovery begins to take place, the patient participates in village activities and does work such as farming or plying a skilled craft if he has one. Many of the women patients engage in petty trading.

At the time of my visit, aspects of hospital ward supervision were being extended to the village. There was a nurse on duty twenty-four hours a day with an office and books in which to keep notes on all the patients. Medications that had been prescribed at the hospital could be dispensed from this office. A nursing superintendent came down for regular calls and periodically Lambo made rounds.

During the day the patient was brought to the hospital, where he could participate in occupational therapy and related activities, and receive as he might need it, drug and electro-shock treatment and to the extent possible, brief, mostly directive, forms of psychotherapy. Not the least important aspect was a meal in the hospital as part of making sure that nutrition was adequately balanced.

The villages have gained considerably from their participation in the psychiatric work. This is particularly true of the main village which has the same name as the hospital—Aro. In addition to returns from rentals, there have been other benefits such as loans provided by Lambo to permit the building of additional houses, piped water, the establishment of privies and so on.

Looking beyond the immediate, Lambo believes that village centers with adjacent day-treatment facilities can be established apart from hospitals. Thus a comparatively small staff could serve large numbers of patients with only a fraction of the building and maintenance costs required by the standard institution. As psychiatrists, psychiatric nurses, social workers and others in the mental health field are trained, there could be a multiplication of such units until eventually some real meeting of prevailing need was achieved—and done within the realities of native culture.

Like the psychiatrists in Sudan, Lambo is looking at native healers with a serious eye. At present most treatment of psychiatric disorder falls to them, and some are even specialists, having houses with resident patients. Lambo feels that numbers of these are detrimental and should be prevented from practicing as soon as possible. For some healers, however, he has respect and thinks they might be cooperative in a project designed for their education and eventual coordination with a program for extended psychiatric care.

The work at Aro is again imaginative innovation. While it is not sensible to think of literal transplantation, there is much to gain from re-examination of our own society and culture with a question in mind as to whether there are not already existing resources which could be captured more effectively. Are there better patterns for out-patient care than our existing clinics? Can the general hospital, the school, the church, the industrial plant, the union and the professional organization be brought more effectively into participation and sharing in the provision of services? Are therapeutic households and therapeutic communities feasible in this society, or could we change so as to accommodate them in some form?

These are by no means new questions and numbers of efforts are under way to see if affirmative answers can be given. Work such as that by Lambo brings a fresh impetus and it is almost certain that in the next decade, more people in all walks of life will be giving such issues serious consideration as practical matters pertaining to their own communities.

Coming finally to the epidemiology of psychiatric disorder, it can be noted first that this very old type of psychiatric research has recently taken a new turn. From counting the number of cases in hospitals, clinics and other relevant institutions, the shift has been toward estimating the true prevalence of psychiatric disorders whether treated or not. For this purpose, samples have been chosen from populations and then each individual in the sample studied.

The central reason for undertaking such investigations is the hope of discovering something about causes. In other branches of medicine, epidemiological surveys have proved themselves a powerful means to this end. That cholera may come through drinking contaminated water, and that pellagra is due to dietary deficiency are two well-known examples. For psychiatric disorder, epidemiology appears to be one way in which the possible effects of social and cultural influences may be explored. If such disorders can be shown to cluster with consistency among people with certain ways of living, then there is here a lead for pursuing questions of causal relationships.

The studies that have been done are still few in number and all are open to uncertainties because of crude methods, the field being in a pioneering stage of development. There is, however, one conclusion that it seems fairly certain later studies will confirm. Indeed, I would predict that they will confirm it over and over again, throughout this country and in many others. The conclusion in mind is that a major discrepancy exists between the prevalence of psychiatric disorder and the means for dealing with it. The psychiatric services now available, whether in hospitals, out-patient clinics, or in private practice, come nowhere near providing relief for this widespread chronic human suffering—a suffering which is at the same time a source of malfunction and inefficiency in societies that can ill afford it in the world's present struggle for survival.

When I speak thus of psychiatric disorder I am including not only the disabling psychotic forms of illness, but also the psycho-neuroses with their symptoms of anxiety, depression, apathy and hostility, and the psychophysiological disturbances in which strained emotions and unconscious processes set going and maintain asthma, peptic ulcer, high blood pressure and other conditions of this sort. Estimates vary as to the percentage. It is probable that different populations have different characteristics, and it is also evident that different research workers employ somewhat different criteria and methods. The range is apparently from 10 per cent to well over 60.

If these figures are so large as to invite disbelief, one may pause to consider such commonplaces of the present scene as the popularity of tranquilizers, juvenile delinquency, drug use, beatniks, angry young men and the inanities of numerous political decisions usually impelled by a flow of popular feeling. There is also a marked increase in the proportion of aged bringing with it a corresponding increase in the mental disorders characteristic of later life.

In addition to estimates of overall frequency there are, too, some indications of how the frequency varies. North American studies show, for instance, that the lower people are in the socioeconomic scale of things, the greater appears the prevalence of psychiatric disorder. It is also evident that availability of treatment facilities has an inverse relationship to socioeconomic position and that except for custodial and organic types of care, those in the lower reaches get virtually no treatment at all.

This means a vast population almost unknown to psychiatry. What little work has been done suggests that methods effective in the middle and upper ranges of money, prestige and education do not work here. Attitude, belief and patterns of human relations are different; and for this reason the need for innovation and adaptation of psychiatric services to these people has some common ground with the kinds of problems faced by Tigani, Baasher and Lambo.

Taking into account both the estimates of overall prevalence and the indications of its distribution in our society, it is not possible to believe that expansion of existing services alone could meet the situation, or even make any significant difference. There is not, for one thing, the qualified personnel to man such expanded services. The existing psychiatric activities in hospitals, medical schools and state agencies are already far short of filling the positions they now have. To create more institutions would be to create new empty shells or to make empty shells out of now functioning institutions by drawing away their staff. A greater proportion of psychiatrists could of course be trained, and no doubt will in the future, but it does not seem realistic to think that there ever will be enough medical schools and postgraduate training centers, nor enough people wanting to be psychiatrists to meet the needs by these means. And, even if, by some strange wave of fashion, such an army of young men and women were to attempt marching through the mills of psychiatric training, society could not tolerate leaving so many other important posts unmanned.

In addition to the question of sufficient psychiatrists, there is also the matter of costs. Although it is hard to make estimates in actual figures, it is surely beyond all reason to think of providing diagnosis and psychotherapy by a psychiatrist according to the prevailing patterns of today to all people with symptoms of psychological malfunction.

High prevalence confronts us again with every one of the issues pointed up in the course of this chapter. The importance of greater understanding and control in genetic processes, in physiological functioning, in psychological transactions and in sociocultural influences comes back for review. Underscored is all that calls in question the present ways of delivering psychiatric services, and the fact that the greater part of psychiatric manpower is concerned with treatment and the teaching of treatment, and only to a very small degree with prevention.

One may object by saying we do not know how to do prevention. There are many ideas and theories, but what evidence have we as to their effectiveness? A partial answer to this is that we do not know very much in a scientific sense about the effectiveness of treatment either.

A further answer is that more is known than is utilized. Of several different kinds of prevention, two, indeed, have been matters of concern in psychiatry for many years. One is the prevention of relapse, avoiding the re-emergence of disability in those who have once been ill. The other is prevention in the sense of early detection and treatment with the idea that more seriously impairing and longer lasting consequences can be reduced. These two are capable of vastly more development, yet to my mind, they are really forms of treatment.

The core idea in prevention is to alter conditions so that illness does not arise in the first place, as in swamp drainage to eradicate malaria. A parallel to this in the field of mental health is the possibility of preventing brain damage. Certain diseases in pregnant women are known to injure the child in this manner, and accidents in the birth process itself, probably through oxygen deprivation, can have similar results. After birth, viral infections and malnutrition may damage intellectual ability and emotional control. Psychological analogues may also be pointed out in the way the infant and child is treated both in the family and in his detachment from the family and movement out to be a member of the larger society. There seems little doubt but that these and other definable events in the life cycle can be customarily transacted in ways which are either relatively safe, or fraught with a high risk of long-range and permanent damage to personality.

The main answer, however, is to say yes, we do not know enough about prevention and to become more fully committed to finding out, to research both applied and basic. Since even the most optimistic outlook on the availability of treatment falls so far short of meeting an emerging picture of need, it is highly probable that the present decade will see just such a development.

To come back to our beginning, the world is being transmuted by its growing knowledge. This is a fast and disorderly process, fraught with both grave danger and dazzling possibilities. Knowledge and practice with regard to mental health are in this flood. There are swelling demands for quicker, more effective, and cheaper treatment and for prevention; these imply major social changes. Information is growing in regard to the genetic, physiologic, chemical and sociocultural bases of disorder and health; this implies reassessment of fundamental cultural values. Because the changing face of psychiatry is part of the changing face of society and culture, it calls for anticipation, forethought, understanding, and planning. Those to be involved include not only the psychiatrist, psychologist and social worker, and not only the geneticist, chemist, physiologist and social scientist who enter the field to conduct research, and not only other medical men, but also lawyers, teachers, clergymen, businessmen, union leaders, statesmen, politicians, civil servants, newspaper writers, radio and TV men, community leaders and ultimately community members of every cast. They are necessary if the potentialities for health are to be realized, and if change is to be managed without geometric progression toward individual and social chaos.

Change through turmoil is, of course, mankind's common history, floundering in a welter of expedient solutions, many of them mutually incompatible. But the problems which confront us today are at root the problems we have raised through increasing knowledge by collective effort, and it is not likely that they can be solved through individualism, ignorance or by looking the other way. As our Judaic predecessors said long ago in the form of a story about a man and a woman, knowledge brings with it responsibility for good and evil.

The Impact of the Natural Sciences
Upon Natural Selection

Jonathan E. Rhoads

TONIGHT WE HAVE TWO SUBJECTS TO DISCUSS—ONE, A TITLE OF MY
own selection: "The Impact of the Natural Sciences Upon Natural Selection," and the other the title of the Benjamin Franklin
series for this academic year: "Machines, Leisure and Culture on
the Eve of the 'Sixties." While the first was selected as a facet of
the second, I have felt an obligation to allude to some of the
broader aspects of the series-title from the standpoint of the
natural sciences. To a great extent it has been this area of learning which has created the machines from which our new leisure
stems—leisure which in turn permits great changes in our culture and no doubt requires some of them.

It is my plan, therefore, to begin with the specific title, then
turn to the generic title and finally to draw the two together in a
few speculations about the future.

As the people of the United States and of the World enter the
1960's certain questions keep recurring in our minds and in expressions uttered all over the world. Among these is the following: If advances in the social sciences do not keep abreast of the
advances in the natural sciences, will the human race destroy it-

self? This question stated in various ways, implies that study of the natural sciences is doing something drastic to survival values, as they have been known in the past.

The title for our consideration tonight, "The Impact of the Natural Sciences Upon Natural Selection," was chosen in the centennial year of Darwin's *Origin of Species,* published in 1859. Traditional concepts of survival value were set forth in part in the *Origin of Species* and were further elaborated and tended to jell in the years that followed. Granted that sufficiently wide genetic variation occurs and that it can be inherited, the doctrine of the survival of the fittest is almost a truism.

However, we must note that this doctrine has two components: the individual who is to survive and the environment in which survival is to take place. We must, therefore, ask, "Fittest—for what?" If the answer is "Fittest for the environment in which the individuals comprising the species find themselves," it would appear that by changing the environment the whole direction of natural selection might be changed. Through developments in the natural sciences we are seeing just this phenomenon. The environment of the human race is being changed and to the extent that this occurs the natural sciences must have an impact on natural selection.

Let us take a few examples. Our past environment has been favorable to species that are quite sensitive to ionizing radiation. The gradual disintegration of radioactive isotopes over the ages plus the atmospheric shielding from the rays of outer space have placed us in an environment in which exposure is low. With the detonation of A-bombs and H-bombs numerous radioactive isotopes are produced. One example is radioactive strontium which can be formed by thermonuclear blasts and distributed widely in the atmosphere. From there it settles or is washed by the rains down to earth and enters our soil. In due time it is incorporated in wheat, a species of life that is apparently more tolerant to it than man. Since it resembles calcium chemically, it is gathered in the bony skeletons of the animals who eat the wheat, including the greatest wheat-eater—man. The half-life of strontium 90 is twenty-five years. It emits beta rays. It remains for long periods in bone where its rays are destructive of the blood-forming elements in the marrow cavities and probably have some power of producing malignant cell lines, possibly by bombarding genetic material in nearby nuclei. While authorities differ, some believe that United States grown wheat already has 40 per cent of the level of strontium 90 which can be ingested with safety.

We think of the obvious implications first: a thermonuclear war, a general rise in Sr^{90} to a level that would kill the human race. Under these circumstances the intelligence that developed the H-bomb suddenly takes on a negative survival value and the dominant species on earth becomes some simpler form of life, capable of standing more radiation and incapable of thinking up ways of destroying itself.

However, we can think of lesser disasters which might occur. Even these would have far reaching effects. Let us suppose that the Sr^{90}—level goes up, moderately, or that estimates of our tolerance for it are reduced. Those foods that contain it in highest concentration would be proscribed. Perhaps wheat farming would cease, wheat farms would be for sale cheap, wheat farmers would be on relief by the thousands, and a part of the farm-equipment business would be gone.

Let us assume that mankind will manage somehow to avoid species suicide and let us explore some of the other possible effects of the natural sciences upon our environment, three especially: the population explosion, the trend toward increasingly complicated organizations as the frame for work, and the excess of consumer goods.

The health sciences have been bounding along from one discovery to another in a way which is perhaps as impressive as that of the physical sciences, though less spectacular. The life insurance tables give a quick overall picture of the net result. In the United States registration area the average expectancy of life at birth was under fifty years in 1901; in 1930 it was up to fifty-nine years; and in 1959 it was up to seventy and a half years. If one goes back further it is clear that the change is far greater than these figures reveal. Indeed one has only to walk through an old cemetery as I did once near Beaufort, South Carolina, to find that more than half of many families were buried in infancy and childhood, only a little over a century ago.

In 1931 statistics from India indicated life expectancies at birth as low as twenty-six years. The impact of adequate nutrition and of better medical care, the elimination of much epidemic disease, and the multiplying of devices that in the aggregate make for easier living—all developments rooted in the natural sciences—are resulting in what is called the population explosion. Within my memory the population of this country has grown from less than 100,000,000 to nearly 180,000,000, and the populations of the world to an estimated 2,689 million in 1955.

Granted a continuance of present birth and death rates, this growth will follow an exponential curve and within several generations, the earth will be very full of people indeed. If the population doubles in 60 years, it would reach eight times its present size in 180 years, i.e. in 2140, and about the end of the third millennium would have advanced 16,000 times more to a figure in the vicinity of 350 trillion, or one person for every five square feet of the earth's land surface.

We do not need to make so distant a projection, however, to see the interrelationship between technology, population and what it takes to get on in the world. Bearing in mind that the causes of the "population explosion" stem from the natural sciences, let us consider by way of comparison the qualities useful for survival that have appeared in less burgeoning populations than our current one. Before doing so it should be pointed out that the term "survival" has several connotations and it is being used in more than one of them in this lecture. First, it is used to mean life versus death of individuals; secondly, it is used to imply persistence of a social structure, such as a nation or a cultural pattern.

Likewise in thinking of evolution we think not only of the survival of one of several genetically distinct species but also of the emergence of a national or cultural or other social group within a species to a more dominant or important position. We must recognize the great degree to which man's adaptability influenced by cultural forces can change him within his present genetic capabilities.

The American Indians are thought to have numbered only 100,000 in the United States. They needed great physical strength and cunning to catch game. They apparently devoted considerable time and effort to warring with each other, and to this end they had formed tight social units in their tribes and somewhat looser federations or nations.

The early American pioneer found himself in an environment that emphasized somewhat similar survival values. Again strength, coordination, endurance, and cunning were qualities essential to success. He was, of course, the beneficiary of much more advanced technology which gave him tremendous advantages over the Indians.

Let us jump now to the prototype publicized by Horatio Alger. Here we typically had a town dweller. Again stamina and energy appear to have had great survival values. Advanced physical skill was seldom a factor. Intelligence of the kind generally applicable to formal education had become important. Acceptance of and adherence to a moral code including pecuniary honesty were stressed as important. Cognizance of the social structure in the American sense, with the hero often marrying his boss's daughter, appears. If these can be taken as reflecting to some extent American experiences in the nineteenth century, they show a heightening of the value placed on qualities which enable people to succeed in a group rather than on those which enable them to succeed alone or as the heads of single families.

Let us skip again to World War II and study what factors had survival value for individuals and for nations. So far as individuals were concerned, the unfit were more apt to survive than the fit because the latter and not the former were useful in military operations and hence, so far as the males were concerned, they were the most exposed. So far as nations were concerned, positive factors seem to have been population, industrialization, organizational and technological genius, plus, in some sense, a peaceful posture before the war which led adversaries to discount too much the military potential of the peaceful nation. To all of these one would add morale.

Broadly speaking it would appear that a combination of manpower and natural resources with technology and human organization determined victory. Great skill in human organization was clearly of high importance, and many observers believe that this was reflected in the selection of Eisenhower as Commander in Chief.

Looking at the players on the human stage, David Riesman, writing in *The Lonely Crowd,* describes three types. The first is the tradition-directed, such as the American Indians of the seventeenth century. The second he calls the inner-directed, caricatured perhaps by the heroes of Alger's fiction, and typified by such figures as Rockefeller, Edison and Ford. Adherence to a set of values acquired early in life and great self-reliance as adults characterize members of this group. Riesman's third category is the other-directed, typified by the younger generation of modern suburbanites, sensitive to styles and trends in dress, manners, thought and action, and responsive to them. He sees the new type as concerned more with consumption than production, buying than saving. It is impossible to know the ultimate validity of Riesman's interpretations and projections, but he has certainly assembled an amazing galaxy of evidence that a major change is taking place.

Let us turn for a moment to one very simple response to the population explosion and the technological revolution which has accompanied it—automobiles. The first car in our family needed no license except for a leather tag required in the confines of Fairmount Park. Soon registration was required, then drivers' licenses, then examinations for drivers' licenses, then automobile inspection of now increasing rigidity, then regulations withdrawing licenses for infractions of rules and, next year, for failure to pass certain physical examinations.

On busy expressways, the maverick driver is now the rare exception. Nearly everyone drives close to a uniform rate. We think of our University motto: "leges sine moribus vanae." Here on the highways both the customs and laws are dictated by the population explosion, which, of course, has been much more rapid for the driver population than for total population. Those pioneer spirits of the highways so familiar thirty years ago are rapidly being driven from the busy areas both by police action and by traffic accidents. Steady, uninspired, legal driving appears now to have a greater survival value in the metropolitan areas than the extra-fast driving which saves a few minutes each trip.

In the field of health the natural sciences have made it possible for individuals to survive who have far less capacity to resist exposure and infections than their forefathers had. Diabetic children

89

can grow to maturity and reproduce. Thus generations of persons are coming into being which are likely to include many vulnerable individuals who would succumb, were the safeguards and helps of modern living, public health and medicine suddenly to be withdrawn.

As older survival values become less important, others gain in *relative* importance; and as the population density increases, some values increase in *absolute* importance.

At present the ability to get a job may not seem to have survival value of much importance in the United States, since the citizen who goes on relief and simply breeds freely may do fairly well in the Darwinian sense. Actually, however, such individuals must be in a small minority if the economy is to remain stable; so I will use the ability to get a job as some measure of the ability to survive in the modern world.

What qualities do we value for employment? Recently we advertised for secretarial assistance in a Philadelphia paper with a circulation larger than *The New York Times*. There were no inquiries from would-be employees. About the same time the College of Physicians of Philadelphia advertised for a janitor, a position requiring little skill. There were 512 inquiries. What does this mean? It would appear to mean that the secretarial skills enabling a person to fit into a large group or become what might be called an organization-woman were in extremely short supply, whereas the willing helper with cleaning and light physical work was a drug on the market. The salary offered was somewhat higher for the secretary.

Turning to another sphere of activity, how do we select men for surgical training? We have been through this process during the past two months, as I write. If there were a field in which Riesman's inner-directed type might seem to belong, it could well be surgery. Yet more and more I find my colleagues and I are afraid to take on the man who does not get along well with his superiors, his peers, and his subordinates. Medical practice in general and surgery in particular have come to involve large numbers of people.

There are on the staff of our hospital more than 300 physicians. There are about 1300 salaried employees. Over 22,000 patients are admitted each year. Poor relations between one of our surgical trainees and any one of these other persons can be awkward, embarrassing, time-consuming, and generally wasteful of human energy. If there are to be thirty or forty men in training at any one time, is it any wonder that social values, the ability to get along with other people and to contribute to a high morale are important? We are still willing to stretch a point for a genius but he must be very productive—and he may crack up psychically in the attempt if he gets too many people working against him.

In industry we have still more vivid examples of the way in which advances in technology, stemming out of advances in the natural sciences, have forced upon thousands of people a network of human relationships. The success of individuals entering this field is now primarily dependent upon their capacity to live in this social framework.

In industrial organizations it seems more and more that the man who can help others work together builds the biggest units rather than the man who is the genius as an autocratic manager. Thus General Motors under Alfred Sloan outstripped Henry Ford's organization and pulled steadily further ahead until the latter's reorientation under Henry II. The largest of American corporations, the American Telephone and Telegraph Company, has recognized the changing times by spending many hundreds of thousands of dollars in experimental educational programs for its younger executives. The most extensive of these programs has been conducted at the University of Pennsylvania under the title, "The Bell Telephone Course in Humanistic Studies for Executives." This was a frank attempt to give mature men, usually in their fourth decade, who had already demonstrated capacity for success in business, a fresh orientation in fields away from technology and business administration in the hope that it would generate people of greater vision—of greater competence in planning for and solving the problems of the future.

Modern technology has also resulted in a situation in which, despite the population explosion, supply of products exceeds demand. For the present we are threatened more by overproduction than by want. Presumably there must be an endpoint somewhere, beyond which the earth and the accessible universe cannot support more people. However, this may be further off than most prophets would suggest. We now have synthetic clothing and some synthetic housing, but we have not yet entered the period of synthetic food on any broad scale. Presumably we will.

One of the results of overproduction made possible by the natural sciences, is to enhance the value of those in the population who can stimulate consumption. What kind of people are they and what are their strengths? They are the salesmen: friendly, outgoing, optimistic, facile in conversation, keen on knowing and remembering people; and the good ones at least are usually sincere. They tend to be other-directed in Riesman's classification, responsive to what other people say, sensitive to what they are thinking.

Another group who are in demand are those unfairly referred to as the "hucksters," the Madison Avenue men: the managers, technicians and artists of the mass media of communication.

Still others are the vendors of credit. The pawn shop has largely been replaced by the installment plan, by the bank loan secured only by the borrower's job and life insurance. Bankers who used to preach frugality and savings now budget funds for advertising and use much of it to stimulate the public to go into debt. This is all part of a pattern to help consumption keep up with production.

To summarize the points which have been illustrated thus far: there seem to be at least three forces which are bringing about a change in the scale of survival values of human characteristics. All of these forces appear to be placing emphasis on those qualities which enable individuals to work together successfully rather than upon those qualities most needed for going it alone.

The first of these forces is the increase in population which has resulted from technical advances (based in the natural sciences) which provide more shelter, more heat, more power, more food, and tremendous advances in the field of health. The population trends appear so pronounced as to justify the term "explosion."

The second of these forces comprises the technological advances, again based on the natural sciences, which necessitate group effort in industrial production and distribution, in hospitals, law offices, in group medical practice, and elsewhere.

Third, there is over-production, resulting from these technical advances, which has made it necessary to attract more and more people into sales and to reward more and more highly those qualities which help stimulate sales whether by direct contact, through mass media, or through financial institutions which enable people to buy before they have earned.

Let us turn now to certain of the broader aspects of the theme of this series: "Machines, Leisure and Culture on the Eve of the 'Sixties." Previous speakers have presented other facets of the subject. The contribution of the natural sciences has, of course, been basic to the developments suggested by this title.

Human muscle as a source of mechanical power has long since been supplanted as a primary source of crude energy. The process of supplanting it in various forms of light work will no doubt continue.

Machines have also reduced the need for skilled work. Thus

much cabinet-making including wood carving is done by machine; music is reproduced by machine, reducing the number of performers needed; photocopying devices are reducing the work of clerks—to cite a few examples. Machines have now invaded the field of intellectual work. The adding machine and the desk calculator are in almost universal use. The electronic computers are growing in capability every year. Not only can they perform mathematical problems of great complexity in unbelievably short time-intervals but they are being used in the synthesis of new names for pharmaceutical products, in the forecasting of election results, in long term weather forecasting—and they may be drawn more and more into decision-making. The various electronic brains in automation devices promise to reduce the work of white collar workers just as the steam shovel and the harvester reduced the work of the pick-and-shovel laborer and of the farmhand.

As these devices for saving intellectual as well as physical labor take over part of their jobs from men and women, what can we do with the time saved and potentially available for leisure? One plan is to shorten the work day, the work week, and the work year. Another plan is to shorten the total years of work so as to allow a longer time for preparation, that is, for study and training.

In this situation we begin to see a cleavage of society along lines of intellectual ability. Those composing the so-called working classes are seeking and obtaining shorter hours per week, more holidays and longer annual vacations. Those going into the professions, including management, tend to work long hours per day, long hours per week, and to spend much longer in preparing for work through study and training. From high school, one can become a factory worker at once; one can train for a few years on the job and become a skilled artisan; one can take four years of college and become a salesman, junior manager, or school teacher; or study six to fourteen years in preparation for becoming a senior manager, a lawyer, college teacher, clergyman, physician or research expert. In higher education we are seeing a trend from four to five year programs in education and in engineering, and from five to six year programs in architecture.

This appears to be a good use of time made available by machines. It is not exactly leisure. It calls for profound shifts in the emphasis of our educational institutions to provide for more advanced study. It also requires methods by which society anticipates the earning capacity of the future student and supports him for a long period earlier in adult life when he does not earn his own living.

The increased application of leisure to learning is resulting in an explosion of knowledge quite as impressive as the explosion in population, but its effects appear to be far less predictable.

Leisure in the more conventional sense is being augmented for the great mass of people in industrialized countries. As longevity increases, more and more persons will have a great lump of leisure at the end of life—say from age sixty-five or seventy for another decade or two. For those with grandchildren nearby, some of this will be absorbed with domestic activities. It is doubtful, however, if this period of life will be attended by much sense of worthwhileness without a basic change in our culture. Satisfaction in being must in some measure replace or at least complement satisfaction in doing.

The effect of both physical and biological sciences on the future is of course unpredictable. However, since the title of this series implies an obligation to predict, I will venture a few guesses, however unlikely.

The technology of war and human destruction has advanced to a point which clearly threatens human and possibly all mammalian existence on the earth. It is entirely possible that there will be an error in management of the new forces. It is even possible that such an error might result in actual extermination of the human race. More likely, however, it would merely exterminate a large proportion of it and would stop short of rendering the earth as a whole completely uninhabitable for man. Under these circumstances the remaining population would, no doubt, build up once again.

These considerations make one think of a verse from the book of Matthew, "Blessed are the meek for they shall inherit the earth." As I was being jostled through the primary grades and grammar school, I often puzzled over this verse. It did not seem to make sense in terms of the world of eight-to-fourteen-year-old children which I was experiencing. In terms of nations or of races it begins to make more sense. One can conceive of those peoples whom history might describe as fierce or aggressive, getting into a conflict in which they largely exterminate each other. If this occurred, nations which history might describe as unaggressive or meek might indeed inherit the earth. Thus the advances in the natural sciences could so alter survival values that the central teachings of Buddhism and Christianity might emerge as dominant patterns for survival.

We must recognize that one of the greatest forces for political cohesion is the fear of other political units—at least it always has been so. It is easy to imagine that all of the areas of the world might gradually be assimilated into two gigantic federations, each of which was cohesive because of fear of the other. Whether these two could ever be permanently drawn together into a union that continued because of the fear of species suicide, remains unknown.

As smaller political units develop their potential with nuclear weapons, it seems not unlikely that the large powers will insist on controlling the small powers before they gain sufficient potential to be able to precipitate a major conflict. How this will come about is not very clear, and the situation is obviously shot through with great peril. This might possibly be the factor which would lead to approval of a UN arms inspection and control plan. (It is of interest that since I wrote this section France has successfully detonated a nuclear explosion.) With some such plan of control, it is not inconceivable that two large and responsible federations might maintain a balance of power and a fairly stable peace for several generations.

Eventually, however, one is confronted with the population question. The obvious answer to the population question would appear to be birth control. If population is to be restricted without resort to war the point of control has to come some time before the average individual has more than two surviving children who will themselves reproduce. This includes the following possibilities: (1) interference with conception, or birth control; (2) abortion; (3) infanticide; (4) sterilization of the less fit, prior to sexual maturity or after one child. One can contemplate these alternatives from religious, ethical, moral and other viewpoints. Let us contemplate them for a moment, only from the standpoint of survival of the fittest. So long as there were two or more national jurisdictions, the one which played the more aggressive role in regard to population growth might force the others to do likewise. Let us suppose, for instance, that one large populous nation which I will call Polypedia resolutely refused to do anything, but that all the other nations limited their populations to then existing levels. What might be expected to happen? Presumably the population of Polypedia would increase and at some point the standard of living there would go down. One possibility is that the Polypedians would emigrate and take up more of the earth's crust elsewhere. If this was not permitted peaceably, the

Polypedians would reach the point at which war would almost certainly occur.

These and other thoughts lead me to the conclusion that population control by any of these methods—and perhaps only birth control would be widely acceptable—will never be enforced continuously except by a world-wide government, or conceivably by mutual agreement and universal enforcement by two or three large federations that agree to follow the same pattern.

Again if one nation began systematic selective breeding, allowing the more intelligent or the more aggressive to reproduce at a faster rate than others, might it not force another nation to do likewise? If various nations began to breed for different characteristics, a new form of competition would emerge.

Eventually it is not inconceivable that some future society might tamper with its own genetic materials, possibly providing mutant strains. Is it conceivable that one such strain might supersede the human race? If so, would this be good or would it be bad? I will seize on this riddle as a place to stop and attempt a brief summary.

Our world, as we enter the 'sixties, is in a state of rapid change. The natural sciences, especially biology, chemistry and physics, have had effects which have gone beyond the scope of the imagination of men who have lived and lectured before. We live amid an explosion of knowledge easily measured in years and an explosion of population easily measured in decades. The impact of the natural sciences is to change the environment of man, so that the survival values upon which natural selection has depended are radically altered. Thus, we see a real risk that man's ability to learn, which has stood him in such good stead in the competition for survival, may now conceivably be his undoing. If this is avoided, we see that the set of values which determines the success of future individuals is changing fairly radically.

It is important to remember, however, that man is endowed with a mind and character, which themselves are the product of natural selection. It would not seem likely that these could change as rapidly as the new environment is changing. As new ways are found of forecasting the future, the human mind is often burdened with fears it may never have been fashioned to face.

Even though genocide is avoided and population growth is ultimately controlled at an acceptable level, the problem of developing a culture—that is, a set of values—which will make our machine-made leisure deeply satisfying, confronts us. To accomplish this great change, I believe we must look to the social sciences and particularly to the humanities, as well as to biology and the physical sciences basic to it.

Problems Facing Architecture

Eero Saarinen

THE STATE OF ARCHITECTURE IN THE UNITED STATES TODAY IS ON A very high level from many points of view.

Modern architecture, which for a long time struggled to win out over false and outmoded eclectic and academic and traditional styles, has won a decisive victory. Today, there is hardly ever even any discussion about whether or not a building should be modern.

Unlike painting and sculpture, which are treated a little bit like outcasts by society, architecture seems to be working in sympathy with society and is accepted as expressing the aspiration and fulfilling the needs of society. The architect himself has come into increasingly higher esteem as a professional in the public mind; in fact, in some poll that was supposed to show how the public respected various professions, architects rated high in the upper levels—complete parvenus in such strata!

Especially, since World War II, there has been a fabulous amount of building in America. In dollars, it amounts to Three-Quarters of a Trillion. This boom has included all kinds and types of building.

Corporations and universities have been among the outstanding clients, and they have chosen extremely well among available architects when they awarded their commissions. The idea that

101

a well-designed building is desirable and that it enhances the corporation or the university has become an accepted idea. The phrases "prestige building" and "showcase building" have entered the clients' language. Good modern architecture is something that these clients are proud of.

Within the professions, we have been fortunate in America in having had with us two of the three great men of twentieth-century architecture: Frank Lloyd Wright and Mies van der Rohe. Standing at opposite poles with their visual language they have stirred up an interesting and healthy discussion and controversy. Much of this has translated itself to enthusiasm for the art of building. Schools of architecture in America are on a very high level today and they produce a dedicated group of young men. And incidentally, it is my impression that your school of architecture is among the four or five best.

There is always a large majority of mediocre buildings in any period. But considering the enormous amount of building in America since the last war, the percentage of well-thought out— and certainly well-intentioned—architecture is extremely high.

Since all these things are true, we might simply say that architecture is in a good and healthy state and this could be the end of my speech. It could be, were it not that I have some grave concerns about architecture today. They are concerns which affect us —the architects—and they are concerns which affect you—the public. And it is about these concerns that I wish to speak to you tonight.

These concerns center on two themes, and these two themes will become the two chapters of my speech tonight. *One* is the problem of principles underlying the seeming confusion of architecture today; the *second* chapter is the narrow concept of architecture.

So, therefore, Chapter One—

102

PROBLEMS FACING ARCHITECTURE

In order to clarify what I mean by these architectural principles, it is necessary to go back historically and set the time and place for the scene today.

The modern architectural movement began just before the turn of the century, parallel to and caused in part by the industrial revolution. In itself it was like a revolution seeking to destroy all ties with the immediate "degenerate" past. Its leaders saw this new architecture eventually forming a new style of architecture, just as other cultures had formed styles—Greek, Romanesque, Gothic and Renaissance. It set out bravely. Because my father was one of the pioneers of this world movement, I remember from my early childhood in Finland the hopes and expectations and the almost religious dedication to this brave new world. The battle has gone through many phases.

First, the functional, where it was believed that a new architecture could be created just by following the needs—the program—and out of this came an over-simplification and the making of a catch-word out of Louis Sullivan's remark, "Form follows function," a remark far more profound and meaningful than is usually understood.

Then there were the corollary, almost moralistic beliefs that great architecture could be created out of honesty toward structure and material.

The so-called "International Style" developed out of those beliefs.

The second phase began around the early 1940's when the emphasis shifted. Where once functionalism had been the front man—the thing architects depended on to make architecture—now structure took first place. It was believed that architecture would automatically derive from the honest expression of structure. At this period, there was also increasing awareness of our time—of the new ideas, of the new science, above all of the new and exciting potentials of technology and industry for architecture.

To sum up, I would say that the three great principles of modern architecture had evolved, three fundamental tools for the new style:

1. Functional integrity
2. Honest expression of structure
3. Awareness of our time.

Tools alone do not make architecture. There must also be leadership to show the direction and this the new architecture had in three great men—Frank Lloyd Wright, Le Corbusier and Mies van der Rohe.

These are the great leaders, their influence together with the three principles is what has created the forum of our architecture. Mixed together, they make the broth which is modern architecture. In different parts of the world, the ingredients of the broth have different proportions. For instance, architecture in South America and Italy is primarily made up out of the fundamental principles plus Corbu. This forms a different product than that of the United States which has primarily Mies, comparatively little Corbu, and FLW as a spice.

In the 40's and early 50's Mies was the overwhelming influence for the United States. The followers of Mies codified his style into a very simple vocabulary of architecture which was to have universal application.

American architecture has temporarily reached a comfortable, simple plateau. It could have jelled into a style which could have become the style of our century with only refinements remaining to be done during the second half of the century.

Was this what the founders of the modern movement had

dreamed about sixty years ago? This was the problem that faced us—the second generation.

Any second generation has both advantages and disadvantages. You can think of the two generations as the one which makes the beachhead landing and the other which has to do with colonization. The first generation is fired with idealism and a clear adherence to revolutionary principles. Its members have to hang together lest they hang separately. The second generation can relax. It can explore. Its members can strike out in different directions. And it can reexamine and question the actions and principles of its predecessors.

The second generation—the one to which I belong—did not want to rest on the beachhead. We did not see the refinement of the Mies style as the final and only answer to the architecture that was to serve our complex society.

That so-called "style" which had developed was much too narrow. It had been codified too quickly and too materialistically. This style saw the different problems of our day all fitting into the same glass and aluminum box—an airport, a skyscraper, a girls' dormitory—all looking the same. There was more to architecture than that. We refused to stop. We felt that there must still be time for searching.

We saw that many interesting things had not been explored. There were new and significant things to be done in structure. The whole science of concrete thin-shell construction was developing exciting new possibilities. The creative engineer, such as Nervi and others, also emerged at this time. There were new and unexplored materials. Concrete and its prefabrication had hardly been explored and promised to open up a whole new form world to architecture.

There were new things coming out of Europe and Asia in Le Corbusier's later work, where the wider vocabulary of the master had not narrowed down the concept of the style but encouraged its broader development.

Above all, the challenges of the great variety of problems to be solved seemed to indicate a greater variety of answers than the so-called "style" of the 40's tolerated. So, the comfortable plateau was abandoned and a new era of exploration into the search for architectural principles and form began. This is where we are today.

Now, let us examine the principles which guide us—or at least a large serious group of us. First of all, we believe unswervingly in the three principles which led the first generation: functional integrity, structural integrity and expression and fitness to our time. These are strong and great principles that we must never forget. But our generation sees that these are not the only principles that have guided architecture through the ages. Two other principles seem to me of paramount importance.

The first of these concerns the significance of the building. When one approaches an architectural problem, one must try to decide what the essence of the problem is and how the total structure can capture that essence. How can the whole building convey emotionally the purpose and meaning of the building?

Now—it is true that not all problems have an essence or an inner meaning—but some do. The problem of a chapel is an obvious one. Imagine what Chartres Cathedral would look like if the Gothic master builders had not placed their main effort on the inner meaning and emotional impact of this building but instead had concentrated their whole effort on making the plan work functionally.

But inner meaning is not confined to obvious examples like churches. It is a problem in all sorts of buildings. For instance, the new jet airport for our nation's capital should also convey its purpose by its architectural expression. The excitement of travel and the stateliness of belonging to the federal capital should be conveyed. A research center for a mass-production industry should communicate its purpose and atmosphere through its architecture. And so on.

Many of our generation believe that the conveying in architecture of the significant meaning is part of the inspirational purpose of architecture and one of the fundamental principles of our art. Therefore, we would add it to the three great principles, or pillars, which we adopted from the preceding generation.

The other significant principle which we would add is concerned with a building's relationship to its environment. Architecture is man's total physical surroundings. In a sense, architecture begins where nature stops. Among leaders in architecture, Frank Lloyd Wright did the most in finding a harmonious relationship between nature and architecture. He showed us how strongly, for instance, a dominant rocky nature can influence the form and character of a building closely related in space.

But there is also man-made nature, man-made rocks. For instance, there are college campuses where the surrounding structures are permanent neighbors. We believe that the single building must be carefully related to the whole in the outdoor space it creates. In its mass and scale and material, it must become an enhancing element in the total environment. Now this does not mean that the building has to succumb to the total or put on the false dress of the past. Any architecture must hold its head high. But a way has to be found to unite the whole, because the total environment is often more important than the single building. So, concern about the building's relation to its surroundings is the fifth principle, or pillar, which guides some of us today.

Now, I believe that adherence to these five principles is important and essential for the creation of good architecture.

But it is true that these two new principles can lead—and have led—to a great variety of architectural expressions. In conveying the inner meaning of the vast number of different kinds of buildings which a society as complex as ours demands, there are bound to be divergent and different expressions. And in adjusting buildings to many different kinds of surroundings, both of nature and of man, there will be very different kinds and types of solutions.

To the layman, this may seem like confusion, but if one looks back to the underlying principles, these different kinds of expressions will be understood not as confusion but as a rich variety.

The trouble is—and now I return to the first of my grave worries—that perhaps we do not always adhere strictly to the principles. With the relaxation and freedom that come to a second generation, the principles no longer stare us in the face the way they did the first generation.

There is much building today which fails to live up to one or two principles, where the structural expression has been ignored, where the responsibility to surroundings has been ignored, or where some other tenet has been violated. One sees cases where a form has been developed for a certain purpose and place with structural significance and justification. Not so very long after this building has been published, this same form appears on many other buildings out of context, and we might say out of "principle."

Our period must be regarded as a period of exploration and experiment, and many avenues of aesthetic expression have been explored, among these, for instance, the surface texture of a building—at times our generation has gone further and flirted with decoration. Architectural decoration is something all historic styles have had—why should we not also have it? It is a good question and eventually decoration may become a part of our architecture. But it is something that will grow slowly, and gradually come out of structural element and structural expression. It cannot be applied and its evolution cannot be hurried. It is a terribly dangerous area for architects to be fiddling with. I know, because at times I have come too close for comfort to making mistakes in this direction.

Decoration leads to short lived "prettiness" when it is not a serious organic part of the material and structure of the building. This kind of adventure leads to confusion.

Sometimes our generation has been tempted into doing rather exhibitionistic things where exhibitionism was not called for. This further leads to confusion.

It seems to me also that deliberately personal expression has crept into the scene. In the 30's, personal expression in architecture was frowned upon because architecture was supposed to be a social and completely anonymous art (some even thought of it as not an art but a science).

Personal expression, I believe, is more a matter of degree. It is right and inevitable that each architect gradually builds up certain convictions and, if you will, mannerisms; therefore, his work distinguishes itself from others. However, in our time, I see the beginning of blatantly personal styles where the trademark of the architect is so strong that it obliterates and negates the principle that building should have an expression of its purpose.

Here I have enumerated some of the traps and dangers for the second generation. They were, first of all, the danger of slipping away from the fundamental principles that we have built up, either by neglecting some or by mis-applying form; second, the danger of decoration; and third, the danger of over-personal styles. There are many more—these are just a few.

As architects, we must stick to principles which allow growth and expansion and variety and not stray up paths which lead to confusion. But the public must learn to understand the principles and to discriminate between false explorations and valid enlargements of the architectural vocabulary and form world.

That is the end of my first so-called "chapter."

The second chapter deals with my concern with

THE NARROWNESS OF THE CONCEPT OF ARCHITECTURE

Architecture is a much broader subject than what is practiced today. My father regarded architecture as everything from the design of an ash-tray in a room to the broadest aspect of a whole city, and I regard it so also. Architecture is the sum total of man's man-made physical surroundings. The interior is, in a sense, the microcosm: the city is the macrocosm.

First, let us speak for a moment about the microcosm—the interior. The interior is just as much architecture as so-called "architecture." Its evolution is based on the same principles.

There are, of course, two separate and distinct kinds of interiors, architecturally speaking. There is the interior which is designed as part of a total building (the girl's dormitory building here presents such a case); and there is the interior, such as that in an apartment or a remodeled house, that has little to do with the already existing structure.

First, I want to focus on the category where the interior is designed along with the exterior as part of the total. Ideally, the interior begins with the building itself. It is the logical consequence of the concept of the building, because this concept is carried through every consecutive design decision. It multiplies like the chromosomes in the cell structure in nature. Thus the interior becomes an integrated and supporting part of the total.

Frank Lloyd Wright came closer than anyone else to carrying a concept through to the last interior detail.

Then there is the much more common problem of the interior

that has to be done in an apartment building or a non-custom-built house. Here, too, there must not be any relaxation of principles. These apartments and ready-made houses provide mass-produced, anonymous backgrounds. We carry on today the enthusiasm of the pioneers for chairs and tables and rugs, etc., which express the character of their technology of mass-production. These mass-produced objects, like the backgrounds, are impersonal and anonymous and should remain so. I believe the so-called "personal touch," or the expression of individuality and personality, should come from other legitimately personal and unique objects—such as paintings and sculptures, mementos from travel, flowers, books and so on. I do not believe that we should ever try to soften or "warm up" or disguise the character of mass-produced objects, but that we should keep the distinction between impersonal and personal objects very clear and sharp.

It seems to me that too little progress has been made lately in this field. It seems almost as if the forces of "cutie pie" and warm, soft interiors are winning the battle. But perhaps there is hope—after all, the fins on the back end of automobiles seem to be on their way out. This is not a piece of inside information from Detroit—it is just observation. Vigilance by the architectural profession and the public are needed here as in all the other areas that are architecture. This vigilance should not stop at the interior, it should go to all parts of the interior: furniture, appliances—down to, as I said earlier, the ash-tray.

Now, let us turn to the macrocosm of architecture—our cities. This is the greatest challenge and the largest frontier for our second generation of architects.

When I say second generation of architects, I include the city planners, because, while we have different names, we must think of this as one task under the total umbrella of architecture—as

I defined it earlier—"the total of man's man-made physical environment."

Talking about the city, I am aware that I am doing so in the one city in the United States which has done the most toward rebuilding itself. You in Philadelphia can indeed be proud of the progress your city planners have made. But, don't be so proud that you sit back and rest on your oars.

The biggest job still lies ahead for all of us everywhere. City planning has many aspects, and I am neither qualified, nor do I wish to speak of many of these. I shall only speak of the conceptual visual aspects of the city as a whole.

Just as a single piece of architecture must have a concept which holds it visually together into one single thing, so must a city as a whole have an underlying and overriding visual unity.

To explain what I mean, let us think back to the plan Baron Haussmann created for Napoleon III in the last quarter of the nineteenth century. It was not a plan alone. It was a total visual concept of how the city could be built into a beautiful organism. The characteristics of that particular organism are those of wide boulevards lined with continuous street façades. After the concept came the zoning laws and set-backs and all the legal paraphernalia that implemented this 3-dimensional plan. The result is the beautiful city of Paris—a city which is a work of art with a sense of total visual unity.

Other older cities have their own unities. Sometimes this unity did not grow in the same way from a single planned concept. Sometimes it is achieved simply by the unity of a certain style of building, or use of common materials, or by height restrictions set—in the days before elevators—by the strength of human legs. Some sections of our older cities also once had this kind of visual unity. The American city of today does not have any such unity.

We are about to rebuild our cities everywhere. We have to because they have decayed and have been destroyed by the automobile. The urban redevelopment plans now in progress from coast to coast sometimes have fine answers to a limited problem. But they all have one lack in common: they all lack the vision and conviction of a total visual concept. They have not found for our times what Baron Haussmann found for the Paris of his time: a complete visual order.

Today we have a certain manner of using high towers and low buildings in our urban redevelopment plans. This is really based on Le Corbusier's concept of how a city should look. But very often the way we develop the mold that he created is so diluted and re-warmed that it just does not work any more.

(As an example, your original plan for the Chinese Wall project was a brilliant and beautiful plan. Ed Bacon deserves the highest praise for it. But I am afraid that what is being built does not have the same spark as the original design. I assume it was a case of too many cooks getting into the broth!)

The core of the problem we face today of placing high towers in our reclaimed areas is the vistas between these towers and our ability to enclose or define space with these building blocks. The space between is as important as the towers. We must find some way of making these arrangements orderly and beautiful instead of looking—as they so often do—like isolated teeth sticking up from a gaping mouth.

I suspect that there is some relation between this problem of placing buildings in the city and the problem, for instance, of the interior plan of a house. Some twenty years ago there was great enthusiasm for the so-called "open plan" in our houses—a plan where one space flowed into the next. This was hailed as an entirely new and dynamic space concept. Much was written about it but nothing great and wonderful came out of it.

113

Today many of us have come back to much more "closed" plans, where rooms are really rooms with four walls. I suspect that in the rethinking of the urban picture we might be coming to a similar conclusion—that we may want to place our buildings in such a manner that the result will be more orderly and legible space.

Whatever the answers may be, the challenge to find them is the greatest one we as architects face today. We must find total visual concepts for our cities. Faced with this challenge, this is no time to relax into second-generation complacency.

After the concept comes the implementation. That is a problem which involves the public as well as the profession. The public, too, must think of architecture not in narrow terms, but in the broadest possible terms.

Architecture and artefacts are the tangible and lasting witnesses to any civilization—and nowhere in the world could such remark find better support than in your Philadelphia Museum, which illustrates this statement so well. The pharaohs and the princes and the popes of the past supported and, in a sense, determined the artistic form of their civilization. In a democracy, it is the people who hold the ultimate responsibility. It is up to every individual to sharpen his visual awareness and to care and to act about these problems. His responsibility is not only the personal environment in which he lives with his family— he is also responsible for the total look and character and form of the cities which will be the final witnesses of what our civilization stood for and believed.

The Politics of the New Collectivism

David B. Truman

PEERING FROM THE BRIGHTLY LIGHTED PRESENT INTO THE DIM shadows at the end of the seventh decade of this turbulent century, few things are clear; fewer still are certain. In the realm of politics especially, he who can say with assurance what the shape of things will be at the end of the 1960's is blessed with talents not given to mere men. But if the pattern of American politics cannot with confidence be forecast, we can still discern in rough outline the kinds of alternatives we shall face; we may in some measure be able to anticipate the constraints that our habits of political action may impose upon our options; we may, in consequence, be able to foresee the strains toward change in our political system that those choices can produce.

Politically the decade just ended has been, at least on the domestic scene, relatively tranquil. Whether one assesses the politics of these years as tepid or as happily stable, innovation clearly has not been their gage. Only rarely and marginally during the past eight years has the Administration been obliged by events to place its unmatched popularity in the balance, and still more infrequently has it elected to do so. But if we have seen few political advances, we have also seen few reversals. No clocks have been turned back, except rhetorically. The tensions of the preceding twenty years have abated as the changes associated with them have moved from the debatable to the respectable.

No such years of consolidation await the next Administration, as both candidates in 1960 seemed to agree. The relative calm of the 1950's cannot last for long. Problems are bidding for solution that cannot safely be postponed. As attempts are made to meet them, the temperature of political debate may rise, and the pattern of our politics may significantly alter. These problems will be varied, not to say complex, and to attempt to characterize them with a single label may be rash. Through most of them, however, runs a thread so clearly evident that the cause of understanding may be served by thinking of them together as the problems of the new collectivism.

1

If the term "politics of the new collectivism" is in some degree shocking, it has been chosen well. For the substance of the struggles ahead will be qualitatively new. "Collectivism" was a word of some currency during the New Deal, though mostly among its critics, but its reference now seems dated. The lasting feature of the New Deal, as those who see "the end of ideology" have argued, was its effort to meet the *individual* problems created by industrialization.[1] This was done largely by devices that transferred purchasing power, directly and indirectly, from the check books of one part of the population to the pocketbooks of another. The means were collective, to be sure, but the ends were individual in the sense that they involved a minimum assurance that the "forgotten men" could participate in the private market, as producers and especially as consumers. The "welfare" of this state was essentially private.

In contrast, the new problems are not concerned with benefits individually consumed. The needs they represent are individual, in the sense that all social requirements can be reduced to such terms, but they are needs that cannot be met adequately through the private sector of the economy, through individual and corporate claims on the country's production. Rather they depend on the size of public, chiefly governmental, expenditure and, ultimately, primarily upon taxation in its various forms. The amazingly effective processes of allocation through the price system cannot, in general, provide adequately for such things as clean air, adequate schools, a rationalized transportation system, a high level of basic scientific research, and a guarantee of law and order, domestic and international, to mention only the most obvious matters. Price cannot do so because these things cannot be sold to individuals or because their benefits cannot be denied—or properly should not be—to persons, individual or corporate, who do not choose to purchase them. The problems of the new collectivism are, in short, common problems, requiring for their solution an increase relatively and absolutely in governmental demands upon production, an increase in the public sector of the economy.

One does not have to certify the clarity of Professor Galbraith's crystal ball in order to be confident of this expectation. His concern for the public sector of the economy is duplicated by many recent pronouncements on a wide range of substantive matters. The publications of the Special Studies Project sponsored by the Rockefeller Brothers Fund clearly carry this message, for instance, as do many of the more guarded statements coming from sources like the Committee for Economic Development.[2] Whether the question at issue is education, urban renewal, or national security, a concern for the relative poverty of the public sector of the economy is a common element in a developing debate.

This debate has focused thus far on such questions as the

effects on the economy of various economic and fiscal policies. But questions of economic capacity, important though they are, touch only one aspect of the problem. A more fundamental element is the question of our political capacity, whether our political system is capable of producing decisions that will be satisfactory. Our problem is not simply a matter of what economic policies ought to be adopted. Other questions are at least equally pressing. What kinds of policies can the political system reasonably be expected to produce? Under what kinds of conditions? What alterations in the system may have to take place if more acceptable solutions are to appear? What, to borrow a phrase from the Rockefeller Brothers report, is "our ability to make choices," not as individuals, but as a political system?

The question of political capacity is at the heart of the politics of the new collectivism, and it is analytically separable from questions of economic policy. A rough analogy can be seen in the chronic problem of agricultural surpluses and the levels of farm income. The key question is not whether solutions can be proposed that are in some sense rational. There are many of them, many that are in fact by any standard more rational than those represented by our present annual expenditure of approximately 5 billion dollars in this area. The question is rather which, if any, of these alternatives can become operative policy. Particular governmental choices among alternative monetary and fiscal policies, of course, have their peculiar political consequences and costs. But just as one may ask "Can we do it?" with respect to some specific economic policy—and in the asking and the answering make specifications or assumptions concerning the underlying political institutions and processes—so in facing the broad problem of the public sector we must ask, "Can the system do it?" and proceed to examine the properties of that system.

Beyond specifying the need in the public sector, political analysis can proceed without any special economic assumptions. This applies even to the much-discussed matter of rates of economic growth. Just as a low rate of growth would complicate the political problem, so a high rate, with its accompaniment in at least slightly increased revenues, might make solutions somewhat easier. But those who argue that the question is only a matter of growth, that, if we can achieve an annual rate of 5 or 6 per cent, for example, our difficulties are over, are relying upon highly doubtful premises.[3] The recent experience of New York State is instructive. A 1959 revision of the tax law produced an unexpectedly large revenue surplus, but it also produced a powerful movement for tax reduction. As a result, much or all of this surplus now will revert to individual taxpayers, despite the State's admitted need for increased expenditures in a number of areas. The New York case clearly suggests that the politics of allocating a revenue surplus between the public and private sectors may be just as heated and just as uncertain in the outcome as the politics of *re*-allocating shares in a product that is unchanging or growing at a relatively low rate.

Analysis of the problem of the public share does require another kind of assumption, however—one involving time. For in this realm the decade of the 1960's is not only a convenient period on which to focus one's speculations about change. It also roughly sets the term of our lease upon opportunity. Most of what needs doing must be done soon, although the deadlines obviously vary from one subject area to another and cannot in any case be stated with precision.

The decade is an approximate measure of our available time primarily because so many of the particular decisions to be made are irreversible. They are irreversible, not in the sense that once they are made there is literally no turning back from them, but rather in the sense that human and material resources once expended cannot be recaptured or readily replaced and that the range of choice may be a good deal narrower tomorrow or the day after than it is today. A generation ill-educated cannot be sent back to school; underinvestment in basic research cannot be made up for in a day; land relinquished to haphazard private exploitation instead of being kept for public uses such as recreation cannot easily be recaptured; neglected public transportation systems cannot be rebuilt overnight; urban areas that have been allowed to deteriorate beyond a certain point cannot be restored and can be rebuilt only slowly and at increased cost; and, finally, an international leadership that has declined because it has been supported by inadequate expenditures on military forces, inadequate assistance to allies, and inadequate numbers of talented men cannot be regained by belated recognition and resolve.

By the end of the 1960's these and related matters involved in the politics of the public sector will have moved toward settlement, whether through conscious choice by the mechanisms of our political system or as a result of our "decision" not to choose. Given the character of irreversibility associated with many of these decisions, the time available for making them is by any calculation limited.

2

The urgency imposed by the nature of these decisions has a significant bearing upon the system of political choice and peculiarly upon the sector of popular attitudes. According to much of the accepted myth and ritual of our politics, especially among laymen, this is the pivotal sector. If change is to occur, the assumption seems to run, mass attitudes, "public opinion," not only must accept altered policy once instituted but also must demand it or in some less precise sense must be its source. If the change is profound, large majorities of the electorate must have come, through direct experience or through persuasion, to see the need for it *before* it can be instituted.

If one can assume, as seems to me abundantly justified, that the new collectivism does constitute a profound change, and if a commensurate change in popular attitudes is indeed a prior condition of action elsewhere in the political system, then the prospects for our ability to make choices in the 1960's are not bright. The circumstances of the decade are not likely to be of the sort that will produce sharp changes in mass opinion, and the years it affords are too few for the processes of opinion change, moving at their normally glacial rate, to be a source of confidence.

Crisis, the great solvent of habit and of customary outlook, is the necessary condition for sharp changes in popular attitudes. Such "productive crises"[4] as that of the early 1930's or that of a decade later are not to be counted upon. Deflation on the scale of the Great Depression, runaway inflation, and total war are possibilities, of course, but crises of this sort might in this decade destroy the political system as we know it or so jeopardize its operation as to make all problems indeterminate. In the absence of crisis popular attitudes cannot be expected to depart appreciably from their accustomed pattern except with the passage of time. It is worth remembering, for example, that the New Freedom of Woodrow Wilson, which was not a product of crisis, drew its popular strength from a generation of protest that had reached a sort of climax in the decade immediately preceding his election.

The constructive contribution of crisis, especially in relation to popular attitudes, is not only that it weakens customary thought and action but equally that it can legitimize under a single

121

formula a wide range of actions that otherwise lack popular meaning. The New Deal and the War Effort were symbols that, though they did not eliminate a variety of particular controversies,[5] provided support and a rallying point for changes too specialized or technical to be widely understood in other terms. In the absence of crisis Fair Deals and New Frontiers may appear in the rhetoric of politics, but they are not likely to have much effect upon the range and vigor of popular support. Broad, programmatic remedies do not produce empowering popular responses in the absence of needs that are equally widely perceived.

The principal consequence of the absence of crisis is that the various segments of the problem of the public sector will be dealt with separately, will each constitute a battleground of an essentially unknown war. Only in retrospect, as is so often the case with events segmentally perceived and only partially understood, will these skirmishes likely acquire a popularly accepted collective label.

This prospect of segmental treatment has at least three implications for the place of popular attitudes in the processes of collective choice. The first and most obvious of these is that so far as these settlements reflect broad popular views, as they must in some degree, these views will have to be taken "as is," without much chance of appreciable change. Consequently, they are not likely to facilitate the politics of the new collectivism.

To attempt to characterize the structure and content of these attitudes in a few sentences is perhaps foolhardy. Yet the evidence is strong that, for all but a few people, attitudes concerning matters of public policy are not organized, not internally consistent, but rather are fractionated, imprecise, and frequently mutually contradictory.[6] Only a fraction of the population, for example, can be expected to express consistent opinions on the desired level of governmental services and on taxation. Most will favor maintaining or increasing some public activities and at the same time will favor reducing taxes.

Inconsistency runs deeper than specific policy, however, and has more extensive implications. We are a people who like our patriotism straight, and often rather strong, but our standard attitudes are at the same time profoundly anti-political. We honor a lot of dead politicians, perhaps because their birthdays are occasions for paid holidays, but not many live ones. Especially in those strata of the population where the life chances of the young mark them for positions of respect in the community, we have no tradition that political leadership is an honored obligation. In our secular faith the elected are rarely of the elect, and *vice versa*. Popular conceptions of the appropriate functions of government undoubtedly have shifted somewhat over the past thirty years. But these changes have not been distributed evenly across the social structure and, because they have been associated chiefly with economic benefits to individuals, almost certainly they have not significantly altered persistent anti-governmental assumptions in other areas.

As a consequence of this anti-political outlook, most of us are able to take an almost indecent pride in our lush national wealth and in our cherished standard of living but simultaneously to regard ourselves as struggling under an intolerable "burden" of taxes. In fact, it is significant that the words "tax" and "burden" are so seldom found apart that, like "damnyankee" in certain areas of the Old South, they are essentially a single term. Given the normal human capacity for preclusive self-regard, it would be utopian to expect the revenue collector to be viewed with deep affection, but the picture of the pitiful taxpayer struggling among all those automobiles and television sets strains credulity almost as severely.

The inconsistency of these attitudes and their anti-political, anti-governmental content provide no solid foundation for a reconstruction in public policy. A program developing segmentally and without benefit of constructive crisis would find here at best unsteady support and at worst, if these attitudes are vigorously activated, unreasoning hostility. For a second implication of the segmental growth of the new politics is that, though popular attitudes must be taken as they are, they can be strongly aroused and even momentarily redirected by real or contrived emergencies short of crisis proportions. This has its advantages and its risks. On the positive side an apparent emergency may permit a lasting shift in policy in the guise of a temporary necessity. This is most likely to occur, however, in the realm of foreign policy and, while permitting increased allocation of resources to military and related activities, to stimulate retrenchment rather than expansion in other segments of the public sector. Nevertheless, without the conveniently inept actions of the Soviets, especially in Stalin's later days, and their associated helpful emergencies, shifts in policy of the sort represented by the Marshall Plan, the Truman Doctrine, and NATO might not have been possible.

The negative side of the apparent emergency is not simply that it may not reach to problems on the domestic front or that the opposition cannot always be relied upon for such helpful blunders, but more importantly that the emergency may not be real, at least in the proportions in which it is seen, or it may be exploited in the mode of "fantasy politics"[7] or both. The essential feature of fantasy politics is that the ordinary citizen is aware, often suddenly, of some frightful danger, an obvious evil that he is against, but lacks the means both of defining its characteristics and of assessing proposed devices for dealing with it. Hence he is susceptible to an almost endless variety of essentially fantastic "solutions," the more so as appropriate counter-measures are complex and subtle. This is, of course, the pattern of demagoguery familiar since the days of the Athenian mob. Novelty lies less in the pattern of the response than in the speed and variety of the precipitating circumstances—chief among these is technological change: change that destroys function and leaves a hollow shell of custom or splinters it into sharp and deadly fragments; change that shrinks the world but leaves population masses centuries apart; change that in that misshapen world often tragically compels such masses to grasp for meaning through destructive stereotypes and specious solutions promoted by irresponsible or misguided manipulators.

A productive crisis might provide a rallying formula that could confine fantasy politics within harmless limits. A succession of emergencies not only is unlikely to supply any such barrier but even may create the means of obstructing the development of constructive policy. Segmental treatment of logically related policy problems facilitates obstruction, not only because proposed solutions in each area lack a common legitimizing perspective, but more immediately because each proposal can more easily appear to be incompatible with—or least in competition with—each of the others. Priorities of some sort are unavoidable, of course, even within a coherent program, but a segmental situation, even in the absence of fantasy politics, may lend itself to presenting the degrees of a priority ranking as mutually exclusive alternatives. Thus the debate in the popular arena more easily may take the form of tax reform *versus* economic growth, military expenditures *versus* improved education, increased foreign aid *versus* public housing, and so on.

Hence a third implication of the necessity to deal segmentally with the politics of the public sector is that whether, in the urgencies of the 1960's, we shall be able to make the choices that are called for is a question to be answered chiefly in parts of the political system outside of popular attitudes. Moreover, since these attitudes must be taken as they are and since they are easily susceptible to the politics of fantasy, much will depend upon the capacity of the remainder of the system not only to innovate in the realm of policy but equally to contain and to neutralize reactive responses to disturbing emergencies.

3

The remainder of the system that is thus critical is much more than the governmental structure itself. For the government both reflects and reinforces the properties of the structures surrounding it. This is true of any socio-political system, but it is peculiarly evident in one that must be classified as pluralistic. This is a term that has achieved such currency that it is in danger of losing much of its meaning. Applied to a decision system, pluralism indicates the existence of a variety of units, numerous but far fewer than the total adult population, each capable of making choices of consequence for the scheme as a whole. It designates an order composed of collectivisms, none of which is, consistently and throughout the whole range of its activities, subordinated to another in anything approaching the form of an integrated hierarchy.

The most important elements in this pluralism are, for present purposes, those capable of making choices in the economic realm. Ahead of governmental units, therefore, one must list first the large business corporations, those "non-Statist collectivisms," to borrow Berle's perceptive phrase,[8] that are able, in an economy that bears only a remote resemblance to the classic model of the market, not only to determine within narrow limits the prices of their products, but also to make choices that directly affect such basic features of the economy as rates of capital accumulation and levels of employment. Alongside these but differing from them in some respects are the components of the communications structure, especially the mass media, which, though admirably neutral in many of their operations, rarely dissent from the norms of the corporate community. In addition, one must give prominent position to the labor unions, farm organizations, and a wide array of interest groups whose claims bear upon the problems of the public sector.

These power centers, though they are frequently in opposition to one another, have in common a stake in their own quasi-independent existence. Selectively and, in a superficial sense, inconsistently they may for tactical reasons support an expansion of governmental activities and powers, but the imperatives of the system lead them to resist changes that in relation to the government or to each other appear to restrict their freedom of action. They thus tend in varying degrees to share and to perpetuate the anti-governmental attitudes that are widespread in the population at large. In those cases, perhaps especially in the business world, where a shift in the relative importance of governmental decisions is likely to alter the prestige rankings in the society—as an increased emphasis on the public sector almost certainly would—these attitudes may be held with the special vigor of those who see their ways of understanding the world, their ideologies, threatened.[9]

Thus these actors in the pluralistic scheme are peculiarly the beneficiaries—rarely the creators—of those features of the governmental system proper that constitute its most distinctive attribute, namely, absence of hierarchy and a strong tendency toward fragmentation in decision-making. They are, in the first instance, partisans in varying degrees of the federal arrangement of constitutional powers, which, though not essential to a pluralistic system, facilitates playing the parts against the whole and legitimizes insistence upon specialized claims in the name of constitutional tradition.

A second basic factor, reflecting and in some measure reinforcing the vitality of federalism, is the highly decentralized structure of the political party, decentralized in a good many instances to a point verging on the anarchic. For, if one looks at that aspect of a party that is always most revealing of the structure of power, the form and location of the choice of nominees, it is clear that the locus of power lies at best in the states and localities. Here are the building blocks of the coalitions supporting presidential nominees. Within the states some party organizations have the strength and coherence to make a responsible commitment to such coalitions and to control nominations for the major positions within their borders. More, probably most, are themselves no more than feeble coalitions, at the mercy of a nominating procedure, the direct primary, that puts the prize of the party label up for grabs among a collection of capricious individuals and irresponsible factions. The states employing this system's first cousin, the presidential preference primary, moreover, introduce into the choice of candidates for the White House a comparably unpredictable element.

This decentralized structure means, for example, that over the fortunes of U.S. Senators and Representatives, especially at the nominating stage, no national party organ traditionally has had any degree of control. Combined with the constitutional arrangement of staggered terms for Presidents, Senators, and Representatives, it further means that each of these tends to be in political business for himself. Each is encouraged to take advantage of that peculiarly American electoral phenomenon, the split ticket. Hence, even in presidential years, the local forces responsible for a President's election are not identical to those that put his party associates in the Congress, especially in those many areas where the crucial choice for less important positions is made in the primary of the dominant party. Finally, this party decentralization means that political careers in the United States are little standardized. A known succession of offices can rarely be seen. Presidents, Senators, Representatives, Governors, and the host of lesser figures may come from almost anywhere, with or without training or testing in relevant positions of lower rank, and they may have few qualities in common save a modicum of popular reputation. The system is in turn reinforced through its tendency to make allies few and rivals legion.

For present purposes the importance of the decentralized party is that it is consistent with a pluralistic general system. Since its parts are not integrated and power is highly diffused, it affords a large number of points at which elements in the larger system can take protective action, imposing limits on initiatives that any may regard as threatening.

Given these circumstances it should not be astonishing that at both state and national levels the separation of legislature from executive has political reality as well as constitutional standing. Given the non-identity, even incompatibility, of the political risks of chief executives and legislators, relations between them necessarily are less those of hierarchy, of discipline, than those of bargaining. Although the resources for such bargaining are in some respects distributed to the advantage of the executive, differences in the power bases of the negotiators imply a wide scope for delay, for dissent, and for veto. Thus the bargaining takes place, if not among equals, among near equals.

The reality of the separation of powers and the supporting diffusion of political risk have the further consequence that hierarchy within the executive branch is at best limited. Although complex technicality, the need for secrecy, and the existence of special sources of prestige may peculiarly foster the tendency of the military establishment to take on an "organizational life of its own,"[10] the ambiguities inherent in the relations of executive and legislature, especially at the national level, produce similar situations throughout the structure of departments and agencies. Serving two masters may be hazardous, but, where it is inescapable, tensions between superiors can be so manipulated as to produce a wide if uncertain freedom of action for the nominal subordinate.

These then are the key features of the political system's core—pluralism, diffusion of risk, and bargaining. Its chief elements, moreover, cannot reasonably be expected to change in the predictable future. Any rapid and significant structural rearrangement would depend upon a crisis so severe that its beneficent potentialities in all probability would be outweighed by the likelihood of disaster. Thus the politics of the new collectivism will develop within the limits of the system as we now know it. Consequently the political problems of the 1960's may be peculiarly institutional in that they may overstrain the system's ability to meet inescapable but ill-recognized challenges.

4

What are the deficiencies to which a system of this type is peculiarly subject? What are the vulnerabilities that must be guarded against if response is to take the measure of challenge? They are primarily two: first, the possibility of insufficiently co-ordinated decisions and, secondly, the likelihood of weakness of initiative within the system.[11]

The condition of pluralism, with its diffused initiatives and decentralized decision structures, invites the possibility that segmental choices that are acceptable to those immediately affected will become, when they are taken in ignorance of or without concern for effects upon other matters, collectively intolerable if not disastrous. At the local level, to use a familiar illustration, one can readily see the necessity for limited coordination, through zoning ordinances, of individual and corporate decisions about where to build homes, factories, and other places of business; and it is equally apparent that a similar coordination by traffic regulations is necessary if individual choices concerning how, when, and where to move about in a crowded urban area are not to be totally incompatible. Nationally it is less obvious that uncoordinated individual and corporate decisions to exploit and to enjoy our high-level technology may neglect and emaciate the educational and research base of that productivity. It is not apparent that segmental and decentralized decisions concerning farm prices, wage rates, and manufacturing charges, which are acceptable to the participants and are made with the object of keeping two-sided conflicts at a minimal level, may produce serious inflation. This, of course, is why inflation is one of the most threatening economic symptoms of mal-coordination in a pluralistic scheme. Finally, it is not obvious that concessions yielded to domestic claimants may cripple a diplomatic *démarche* or subject a military or foreign economic policy to futile oscillation.

How serious these prospects of non-coordination will be for a pluralistic system depends fundamentally upon the characteristics of the processes that produce the system's decisions. Inevitably these processes require, for the participants' own objectives, a high degree of skill in negotiation. They require additionally, if bargaining is not to dissolve into unrestrained conflict, the existence of a consensus on the rules of the game, acceptance of legitimate procedures for reaching and enforcing agreements. For the system's survival, however, they require that the consensus also include two other matters: agreement on where the responsibility lies for bringing into the negotiations those considerations of consequences that the parties to the bargain otherwise may ignore and, equally, agreement on the right of such interventions to supersede bargains where the two are not consistent. The principle underlying this last requirement is as old at least as the law of contract and as familiar as an anti-trust suit. The problem is not that the principle is unfamiliar but that its application to different types of bargains is not accepted.

The need for restraints upon bargaining through such intervention is the point of convergence between the danger of uncoordinated decisions and the second vulnerability of a pluralistic system, weakness of initiative. Beyond the possibility that consensus may not include the right of intervention is the more fundamental danger that it may not include agreement on where initiative must lie—within the system in general and within the governmental structure proper—with respect to novel matters and especially those that cannot be dealt with through the processes of spontaneous bargaining, matters typified by the issues of the new collectivism.

Implicit in a pluralistic or individualistic system is the assumption that diffusion of initiative will foster creative action. American experience justifies that assumption, but it also obscures the dependence of that justification upon a specific set of circumstances: the units to which initiative has traditionally been delegated could be counted upon to take the kind of action required by the society because the needs which those initiatives reflected were directly and immediately connected with these units' own conscious purposes. Thus, to put the matter over-simply, when the principal needs of the society were to develop the resources of the continent, delegation to individuals and corporate groups could be expected to produce the required kinds of initiative because in the process their own fortunes were likely to be advantaged. When the society's needs have shifted, however, so that they are no longer primarily of the kind that is met by such direct self-serving, and the pattern of delegation remains unchanged, initiatives will still occur, but they will not likely be the ones required by the new needs. That is, the newly required initiatives are unlikely to be taken because doing so is not essential to the survival, in the short run, of the units of delegation. The stakes are not appropriate. In the simple words of Izaak Walton's wise friend, what is everybody's business is nobody's business.

In the real world a complete absence of initiative concerning such interstitial matters is unlikely to persist indefinitely, of course. With respect to any of the questions facing the society some groups, governmental and non-governmental, make it their business to take the initiative or, more characteristically, to agitate for initiative from the government. In the course of time they may, with the aid of events, achieve a tolerable degree of acceptance of their demands. Considerable time may be required, however, because the basic assumptions of the system are against changing the pattern of delegation. They are against centralization, are non-hierarchical and anti-governmental. Unaccustomed exceptions to these assumptions, threatening both symbolic and material deprivations for important segments of the society, are not readily granted. In the short run the system protects these assumptions through legitimizing the use of the many points at which negative responses to initiative can be expressed and positive action can be effectively stopped. The system tends to permit such responses, to grant them presumptive legitimacy, even though they may take the form of fantasy politics. The mere prospect of such responses, moreover, may easily lead those in governmental positions to avoid attempts at innovation. Unsure of the chances that initiatives on their part will receive supporting responses from the system, or persuaded that they will not, the sources of a possible central initiative may prudently decline to attempt it.

Thus in the short run the system tends toward postponement, toward inaction, toward immobilism. The short run, however, is almost certainly all we have to work with. The challenges of the new collectivism do not carry with them a generous allotment of time.

5

Uncoordinated decisions and weakness of initiative, however, are merely tendencies of the system. Their degree is not a matter of certainty. Just as it is not inevitable that what used to be called the American experiment will indefinitely survive, so it is not inevitable that the vulnerabilities of the system as we know it will prove inescapable. The variables upon which either prediction would depend are not known so precisely. If we have room for speculation, therefore, we may well ask what is required if the deficiencies of the system are not to be realized and what trends can be seen that give some prospect of meeting those requirements.

Many could be listed, but, if the lines of this analysis are valid, two requirements would seem to be fundamental. If, first, uncoordinated decisions and their consequences in the public sector are to be avoided, an increase in the strength of central authority in the system will have to take place sufficient to reduce the diversity of risk within the political structure and thus to restrict the ease of negative action. Secondly, avoidance of a weakness of initiative in the system will require special capacities of those in command of points in the pluralized structure, especially outside the government. These are the elite of the system, those in whom de Tocqueville put his faith when he proposed a means of achieving "many of the political advantages of aristocracy . . . without its injustice or its dangers."[12] In the crucial politics of unseen emergency, they are, for all practical purposes, the people. From these must come awareness not only of the consensus requirements of a bargaining system but also of their own strategic and essentially privileged positions in the system. Such awareness could bring into the bargaining situation restraints going beyond the need to preserve independence of action and capable of containing the threats of fantasy politics. Simultaneously it could provide intelligent, informed support for central initiatives necessary to meet the challenges of the age.

These two requirements are, of course, interdependent. That is, a reduction in the autonomy of the decentralized units of decision would in some measure both reflect and foster elite attitudes permitting strong initiatives and encouraging the containment of fantasy politics. But though they are interdependent, they can be separately examined.

Concerning trends toward strengthened central authority, it is well to remember that typologies such as we have been exploring can be misleading. No real political system conforms precisely to the pure pluralistic type, and all such systems are constantly changing, often without contemporary notice. The American governmental system, which is considerably older than its pluralistic order, has been moving steadily, if unevenly, toward more centralized authority since the days when Alexander Hamilton and his allies at the Philadelphia convention accepted a modified federalism, not as doctrine but as temporary accommodation to necessity. Especially in the present century, as the United States has moved irrevocably from the condition that de Tocqueville described as "a nation without neighbors," the "working constitution" has undergone dramatic change in the direction of centralization.[13] Such change is not astonishing; the proposition is well established that the impact of contact between groups, especially contact involving conflict, alters their internal power structures.[14] It would be unlikely that the contacts and conflicts associated with America's emergence among the nations would not have affected its system of governmental power.

James Madison anticipated in 1788 that "times of war and danger" would tend to give the federal government ascendancy over the states.[15] These are assuredly our times, and, though external threats have not been the only source of change, they have been associated with an unmistakable shift to the center in the federal system. Although our myths have not kept pace and our practices have produced distortions in effect, the power and importance of the central government, however they may be measured, have increased at a far more rapid rate than have the states'. And the trend shows no sign of slackening.[16]

In response and somewhat in parallel, but less clearly and at a slight remove in time, the patterns of electoral politics have shown increasing signs of nationalization. Sectional monopoly of voter loyalties, the hallmark of the decentralized party, is being eroded, and candidates for elective office, especially for the House and Senate, are increasingly caught up in conflicts over national policy. The locus of political risk has not clearly moved from circumference to center, but the stake of the Representative or Senator seems to lie increasingly with the electoral fortunes of the party label with which he is identified. In turn, signs are appearing, though they are neither clear nor consistent, of a drift of influence toward the national center of the formal party structure itself, a drift that might be expected to follow an increase in the prominence of the national political arena.[17]

These nationalizing trends have fostered and in turn have been reinforced by increasingly integrated leadership in Washington. As Woodrow Wilson anticipated more than five years before he entered the White House, the President has become "one of the great powers of the world, whether he act greatly and wisely or not." He is no longer a "mere executive," but the pivot of the whole structure.[18] Integrated leadership, however, has not been confined to the Presidency. His emergence and the conditions that have fostered it have also put into the hands of the party leaders in the Congress, chiefly the floor leaders and the Speaker, the means of containing the centrifugal tendencies of the legislative body. These means are not unlimited and they are not consistently available to the President on his own terms, but their emergence may mark the early stages of a modification in the separation of powers whose importance to constitutional practice in the long run may be of major consequence.[19]

The trends with respect to our first requirement, then, are running in the direction of an increase in the strength of central authority. Whether they are strong enough or have moved far enough to sustain the coming need it is impossible to say, but the direction is clearly apparent.

With respect to the second requirement, an initiative-sustaining self-awareness among the non-governmental elite, trends are not evident, and confidence is much less warranted. In particular it is by no means certain that the corporate community, the crucial element in the supporting structure, will see in the increased governmentalization that is called for by the new politics a necessary modification of the system rather than a subversion of it. Favorable signs appear in the words of a major industrialist who is bold enough to suggest before the annual meeting of the National Association of Manufacturers that Americans in general and businessmen in particular may be paying too little rather than too much in federal taxes, and a similar sort of inference can be drawn from some of the activities of a group such as the Committee for Economic Development. But for every such indicator there are several more testifying to the readiness of various groups, not alone those in the corporate realm, to use the still open features of the system to exact costly concessions and to restrict innovation.

Confidence based wholly on the trends, therefore, would probably be unwarranted. Nevertheless the trends are not unimportant, and they may be exploited in the segmental battles over the new collectivism to produce results that by hindsight may seem remarkable. Not all elite groups need be involved in all such skirmishes, and thus not all need be drawn to the support of central initiatives. Similarly, not all the decision points within the decentralized structure need be contained in any single effort. If by skillful tactics the issues of the new collectivism can be so raised as to cluster them and to influence the alliances that form on either side, potential opponents may be quiet or may be divided and neutralized.

An example of such possible tactical clustering of issues can be drawn from the area of federal taxation, likely to be a central battleground of the new politics. An area of conspicuously uncoordinated decision-making, the individual income tax has been subject over the years to a series of concessions to special groupings of taxpayers, with the result that the tax base has been eroded. These concessions, moreover, may easily be added to, so that the revenue advantages of even an increased rate of growth in the economy may not be fully realized. To attempt to close any one of even the major "loopholes" would be a formidable political undertaking. Thus, to attempt to eliminate the so-called depletion allowance would create a nation-wide defensive alliance among owners of producing property ranging from oil and natural gas to brick and sand. A general revision aimed only at eliminating such concessions would almost certainly augment this alliance without compensating advantages in support. If, however, a general revision intended to close all or most loopholes were combined with a proposal to reduce significantly the tax rates in all income brackets without loss of revenue, which seems to be perfectly feasible, support for this initiative might be generated in sufficient strength to weaken or neutralize the admittedly formidable opposition.[20]

Such an effort would admittedly test the strength of central authority and of elite responsibility. By no means all the issues of the new collectivism, moreover, will be susceptible to such tactics. Events beyond the control of any leadership within the United States may nominate such issues for decision under circumstances that may not augur well for effective action. Given the persistent vulnerabilities of the system, chance will inevitably play a large role in making its record in the 1960's. In particular, how the issues cluster in time will in large measure determine who expects to be hurt by their solution and, in consequence, what combinations and alliances within the system will form to exploit its weaknesses.

The system's "ability to make choices" of the sort that seem to be called for is limited. Exploiting the trends that have begun to emerge in recent decades and using the opportunities that may be provided by favoring fortune, the system could be equal to the challenge, and by hindsight we may see that it has undergone major changes that have modified its deficiencies without destroying its strengths. All that seems certain now, however, is that the governing capacity of the American system will be tried in the decade of the 1960's as severely as at any time in our constitutional history.

139

Notes

1. See, for example, S. M. Lipset, *Political Man* (New York: Doubleday, 1960), chap. 13.
2. John K. Galbraith, *The Affluent Society* (Boston: Houghton Mifflin, 1958). See especially *The Challenge to America: Its Economic and Social Aspects,* Report of Panel IV of the Special Studies Project, Rockefeller Brothers Fund, Inc. (New York: Doubleday, 1958). See also various statements and publications of the C. E. D. on taxation and public expenditures.
3. For example, Leon Keyserling, "Public Weal—And Private Too," *The New York Times Magazine,* August 21, 1960.
4. To borrow a happy phrase from Richard E. Neustadt, *Presidential Power: The Politics of Leadership* (New York: Wiley, 1960), p. 186.
5. Such as the dispute over provisions of the Emergency Price Control Act of 1942 giving privileged position to food products, the less publicized and successful effort of the petroleum industry to prevent any disturbance of the pre-war shares of the domestic market, or the little-known conflict over whether to promote the sale of war bonds as an essential counter-inflationary measure and thus to encourage acceptance of the government's responsibility for managing the economy.
6. See, for example, Angus Campbell, *et al., The American Voter* (New York: Wiley, 1960), chaps. 9 and 10. It can be argued, of course, that these attitudes reflect a perfectly rational distribution of energy resources on the part of the electorate, even though their possible consequences for government may be undesirable. See the suggestive essay by Anthony Downs, "Why the Government Budget is Too Small in a Democracy," *World Politics,* Vol. 12, No. 4 (July, 1960), pp. 541–563.
7. The term is Professor Robert A. Dahl's, in an unpublished manuscript.
8. A. A. Berle, Jr., in his "Foreword" to E. S. Mason, ed., *The Corporation in Modern Society* (Cambridge: Harvard University Press, 1959), p. xiv.

9. Cf. Francis X. Sutton, *et al.*, *The American Business Creed* (Cambridge: Harvard University Press, 1956), especially chaps. 9, 17 and 18.

10. Walter Millis, *The Constitution and the Common Defense* (New York: The Fund for the Republic, 1959), p. 20.

11. These vulnerabilities are present, of course, in any pluralistic system, but they are accentuated in one that also works through a federal governmental structure. On this point see the perceptive essays of Samuel H. Beer, "New Structures of Democracy: Britain and America," in W. N. Chambers and R. H. Salisbury, eds., *Democracy in the Mid-Twentieth Century* (St. Louis: Washington University Press, 1960), pp. 30–59; and Robert A. Dahl, "The Politics of Planning," *International Social Science Journal*, Vol. 11, No. 3 (July, 1959), pp. 340–350.

12. Alexis de Tocqueville, *Democracy in America* (Bradley edition, New York: Knopf, 1946), Vol. 2, p. 324.

13. de Tocqueville, *Democracy in America,* Vol. 1, p. 126. The phrase "working constitution" is from Walter Millis, *The Constitution and the Common Defense,* p. 21.

14. See, for example, Muzafer Sherif and Carolyn W. Sherif, *Groups in Harmony and Tension* (New York: Harper, 1953).

15. *The Federalist,* No. 45.

16. On this point see the stimulating essay by William G. Carleton, "Centralization and the Open Society," *Political Science Quarterly,* Vol. 75, No. 2 (June 1960), pp. 244–59.

17. On these trends see E. E. Schattschneider, "United States: The Functional Approach to Party Government," in S. Neumann, ed., *Modern Political Parties* (Chicago: University of Chicago Press, 1956) and V. O. Key, Jr., *American State Politics* (New York: Knopf, 1956).

18. Woodrow Wilson, *Constitutional Government in the United States* (New York: Columbia University Press, 1908), p. 78.

19. David B. Truman, *The Congressional Party* (New York: Wiley, 1959) and "The Presidency and Congressional Leadership," *Proceedings of the American Philosophical Society,* Vol. 103, No. 5 (October, 1959). Donald R. Matthews, *U. S. Senators and Their World* (Chapel Hill: University of North Carolina Press, 1960).

20. See Joseph A. Pechman, "What Would a Comprehensive Income Tax Yield?" an essay prepared for the use of the Ways and Means Committee of the House of Representatives, republished in Herbert Stein and Joseph A. Pechman, *Essays in Federal Taxation* (New York: Committee for Economic Development, 1959), pp. 17–47.

Religious Issues in Twentieth-Century Culture

Daniel D. Williams

AN ATTEMPT TO IDENTIFY THE MAJOR ISSUES IN RELIGION WHICH
will be faced in the 1960's is complicated not only by the limitations of the writer, but by the many currents of thought and
feeling in today's world. We are in a cultural revolution in which
traditional forms of religion are being discarded, and yet one of
the strong trends in our century is the renewal of loyalty to inherited forms of religious faith and community. Some try to reduce all meanings to scientific terms and dispense with ancient
religious symbols, while others assert that the way to understanding man's existence is through exploring the depths of religious
symbols. There is a world-wide impulse toward the discovery of a
religious unity in which the many faiths can find mutual reinforcement over against the secular spirit, and at the same time our
century presents some of the most uncompromising stands on the
uniqueness and absoluteness of particular faiths, as in Islam, and
in some Christian theologies.

Religion cuts many channels as it flows through man's political
and cultural life. Asian political leaders try to relate Buddhism
and Marxist ideology to see how they can live together. Western

sophisticates discover the spiritual disciplines of Zen Buddhism. A pagan National Socialism exploited the power of religious feeling to create a demonic nationalism, but called forth the resistance of the confessional church and some of the authentic martyrdoms of the twentieth century. In South Africa Christianity is used as a bulwark of the policy of *apartheid,* and at the same time there arises a prophetic Christian protest from within the ranks of the controlling group. Religion can be constructive or demonic, revolutionary or conservative, culturally stimulating or stifling. Therefore, simply to list a number of issues which concern religious people would not be very illuminating. It is more important to ask what has produced the present religious situation, and to see how the issues arise in our common life.

We should be clear about what we are to call "religion." We can say that religion has two aspects. There are the *religions* of mankind. These are communities of faith and practice organized around some response to a divine reality which gives meaning to life and to which men seek to relate themselves. There is also the religious *spirit,* man's response to whatever he holds to be of final consequence for the meaning and destiny of his life. The religious spirit may or may not be expressed within a particular community of faith. At times it may appear as a protest against all traditional forms of religious belief and practice; but we shall say that the religious spirit is present wherever man searches for or responds to something which he takes to have ultimate significance for his life. In the history of religious communities we know that the religious spirit in both its creative and its destructive aspects may appear either within or outside of the traditional forms of religion. It may be expressed as a belief in God or some divine reality, or it may become an iconoclasm or atheism in which all concepts of God are attacked. But it is religious when, in Dr. Tillich's phrase, man's "ultimate concern" is involved. In the twentieth century a tension between the religious spirit and traditional forms of religion is one of the characteristic phenomena.

Dr. Toynbee has said that challenge and response is the key to the history of civilizations. It is also an important key to the history of religions. We can understand the formulation of the major religious issues today by seeing that those who hold some kind of religious faith have responded in one of two ways to the protest against traditional forms of religion. Some have sought to make a creative response from within a religious tradition, the others have sought to find a new religious standpoint beyond the inherited forms of faith.

It is not possible to say that any one element in the life of modern man has been the determining factor in shaping the forms of religious life and thought; but one pervasive factor has been that of modern science and its effect upon man's way of understanding his world. We can well begin by examining the radical new situation created by modern science for religion.

While the nineteenth century and the beginning of the twentieth century are known as periods of optimism in western culture, an undercurrent of disturbance and pessimism grew stronger as the turn of the century approached. Consider these words of Thomas Hardy written about 1900:

> What we gain by science is after all, sadness . . . . The more we know of the laws and nature of the universe, the more ghastly a business one perceives it to be.[1]

Hardy was haunted by the disclosure in Darwinism of the ruthless struggle of life with life. He may also have been thinking, as many were, of the second law of thermodynamics with its prediction of the inevitable dissipation of all useful energy. Hardy thought that modern critical thinking left no place for a belief in God which allowed any anthropomorphic elements whatever. Therefore the world is founded on something impersonal.

What in Hardy was still a somewhat wistful longing for religious assurance became as the twentieth century dawned a blunt protest against all religious faith. In Freud's psychology, religious beliefs are illusions, the projection of frustrated infantile wishes. In the revolutionary protest of Marx, religion is declared to be an ideology which covers up the cleft in the human consciousness produced by a divided and unjust society. This theory developed by Marx in the nineteenth century became a main theme of the world revolutionary movement of communism in the twentieth century. A socialist chess set recently designed by a German wood carver in the East zone has the King's place in the set taken by a worker holding the economic plan in his hands. The castles are figures in the uniform of factory defence squads, and the bishops are athletes.[2] It is a fair symbol of one of the major challenges to religion in the twentieth century.

Intellectual skepticism which seeks to dissolve the religious symbols by rational analysis lives in our century in logical positivism. New techniques in philosophical analysis do not necessarily support the positivist attack on all religious language; but they raise serious questions about the possibility of giving rational justification to traditional beliefs about God or indeed about any metaphysical realities.

Finally there is what may be termed the "humanistic protest" often voiced in modern existentialist philosophies. It asserts man's radical freedom in the universe, but his aloneness. Jean-Paul Sartre says that whereas in the Christian tradition God creates the world out of nothing, the existentialist truth is that man creates his world out of nothing, the "nothingness" of his freedom. He must bear the burden of his own guilt. He must live with courage knowing that his life runs toward death. He must refuse to be reconciled to a world in which innocent children suffer. Friedrich Nietzsche was the prophet of this protest when he proclaimed in his *Thus Spake Zarathustra,* "God is Dead."[3]

When we examine the ways in which contemporary religion has responded to these challenges, we recognize that there are inward springs of religious life which do not depend upon external challenges to give their sustenance to the human spirit: but to understand religious life today we must see how these protests have been met.

There are two main ways open for those who resist the disintegration of all religious forms of belief. One is to stand within the traditional religious community, and to reinterpret inherited faith in the face of new needs and new issues. The other way is to step out from the historical religious community and to seek a new standpoint relieved of the encumbrance of tradition. Which issues one will take most seriously is determined by which of these two ways is chosen. I have put their opposition sharply, and would not deny that some mediating positions are found; but an ultimate choice between one or the other would still seem to be required.

1

One of the most striking features of the situation in mid-twentieth century is the reassertion of the vitality of the great religious traditions. It is a world-wide movement in all the major faiths: Buddhism, Islam, Hinduism, Confucianism, Judaism, and Christianity. It may be called a "renaissance" within the traditions, for it involves a turning to the origins and roots of an historic faith in order to rediscover the enduring truth, and it may lead to a reshaping and reinterpretation of the faith. The key to this movement is the preservation of a heritage through examining, criticizing and reinterpreting its central themes. It involves adjusting traditional beliefs in the face of new knowledge, and new cultural demands. Sometimes this reshaping takes the form of a modernism in which old symbols are given new content. Sometimes it takes the form of an explicit reassertion of orthodoxy; but it is often a "neo-orthodoxy," a re-establishment of traditional forms of belief with adjustments to the new knowledge derived from science and from other cultural sources. The depth and extent of this response from within the traditional religions would probably astonish Nietzsche, Freud, and Hardy, if they could witness it. Some interpret it as a natural consequence of modern man's search for spiritual security in an age of anxiety, and surely this is one factor within the movement, but we need to look more closely at how it is that traditional forms of religion have found such a vigorous contemporary response.

First, this reaffirmation of religious tradition has come as a counter protest against the excessive optimism of modern philosophies of progress. It is unconvincing to say that the traditional faiths have persisted only because they offer a refuge from anxiety. Modern man had an alternative refuge, the hope of endless improvement of his life enshrined in the doctrines of progress. It is this optimistic view of history that the traditional religions attack. They have tended to agree with the more severe critics of modern man's self-confidence, that the establishment of a genuine security depends upon a much more radical appraisal of man's plight as a creature subject to the risks of freedom and self-destructiveness. The traditional religions oppose a simple humanistic self-confidence with their sense of dependence upon a divine reality, their drastic demands for repentance and for self-discipline, and their affirmation of a saving reality from beyond history as necessary to the solution of history's dilemmas.

In the Christian Church it is the polemic against an easy self-confidence which has characterized the creative theologies. The two outstanding figures are Karl Barth, the Swiss theologian who led the opposition of the confessional church against the Hitler regime, and Reinhold Niebuhr, the American theologian whose *Moral Man and Immoral Society* published in 1932 near the beginning of the great depression turned liberal Christian theology back to a radical doctrine of man's sin and guilt. Niebuhr combined evangelical theology with a realistic political ethic in which the tragic conflicts of power, and the limits of human virtue and wisdom in history were interpreted in the context of biblical doctrines of the fall and grace. He argued that the Biblical tradition understands man more profoundly than have the dominant philosophies of modern culture. The theological climate in the 1930's became more sympathetic to the critical voices of cultural protest. As one symbol of this convergence of the cultural mood of criticism from the two sides of the religious tradition and the disillusioned philosophies there is the figure of the lonely Danish genius, Sören Kierkegaard, whose existentialist Christianity was a formative influence not only upon theologians like Barth and Niebuhr, but upon modern Jewish thought, and some Buddhist thought, and was a source of both the agnostic and frankly atheistic philosophies of twentieth century existentialism. Through this movement from Kierkegaard to Sartre in both its theological and non-theological forms, there runs the theme of man's anxiety in the presence of an ultimate risk, the mystery of death, and the burden of guilt.

A second reinforcement of traditional religion has come from the protest against the dehumanizing elements of technological culture. Here again the religious traditions tend to join forces with the secular rebels against the assumption that the extension of man's scientific power will solve his problem. Martin Buber's religious philosophy is one of the most important instances of the religious defence of the person against dehumanization.

Buber writes from within biblical and Hasidic Judaism, as he develops this thesis that the I-Thou relationship between persons is radically different from the I-it relation between a person and an object which is something merely to be contemplated and used. For Buber the I-Thou relationship is the heart of human reality, and it is not possible for men to enter into it except on the basis of a recognition of God and a personal relationship to Him who is the supreme and ultimate subject. Buber's doctrine has influenced not only Jewish and Christian thought, but other contemporary philosophies.[4]

The protest against dehumanization has an especial significance in Asia where there is a recognition of the overwhelming power of scientific technology to reshape the world's life, but at the same time a deep fear of being engulfed by a civilization of technological power without spiritual sensitivity. In Islam, Buddhism, Confucianism, and Hinduism the question is being asked, is it not possible to have the scientific method and the knowledge and techniques it produces, but to join these with the spiritual sensitivities of the religious traditions? Those who see most deeply into this question recognize that this is more than a matter of simply joining two sets of concepts and values to one another. Creative reinterpretation of the ancient faith and of scientific values is required if the two are to be brought into one whole.

Finally, among the factors reinforcing the loyalty to traditional religion there is the fact that man has his religious existence generally within communities of religious faith. Religion creates societies and binds peoples together. It symbolizes collective memories and hopes. Hence it has always been close to the historical forms of collective life, and in our day it is deeply involved in the dynamism of modern cultural nationalism which is certainly one of the most powerful forces in contemporary history. The search of peoples for self identity, and for political power and autonomy inevitably involves the religious traditions which have informed the common life. On the whole the trend of modern nations has been to disestablish religious institutions; but at mid-century there is a strong opposing tendency. Pakistan is an Islamic State; Burma and Ceylon are moving toward some form of Buddhist state. The political tensions in India are in part related to struggles between religious traditions as in the case of the demand of the Sikhs for a separate state. It is significant that communism in spite of its ideological critique of all religion still tends to be cautious in dealing with traditional religion in places where as yet it has no preponderance of power. Even in central Europe, in Poland, and in Russia itself there seems to be a policy of at least minimal toleration of the religious communities.

The motives of political cohesion and national self identity are not the only ones which tend to strengthen the hold of religious communities. There are the motives of personal need for the symbols of religious experience, and for the inspiration of religious faith.

Some English interpreters of the present cultural scene recognize a "Braithwaiteian" religious motivation following the philosopher Braithwaite, who after having taken the position that no satisfactory rational grounds for accepting traditional Christian belief can be given, enters the established church because the religious spirit and the symbols of faith give practical reinforcement to integrity in human living. There are universally significant elements in Boris Pasternak's picture of Lara in *Doctor Zhivago:*

> Lara was not religious. She did not believe in ritual. But sometimes, to be able to bear life, she needed the accompani-

ment of an inner music. She could not always compose such a music for herself. That music was God's word of life, and it was to weep over it that she went to church.[5]

For all such people, within the religious community, or standing near to it, and drawn to it, those who have grown up within and have never left, and those who have been outside and have been converted, certain issues appear which must be faced if the tradition is to be possessed and interpreted for contemporary living. The first of these issues concerns the credibility of religious faith in its inherited forms. How can religious beliefs be made intelligible in the thought-world of the twentieth century?

Skepticism about religious beliefs is a perennial aspect of culture; but it is true that the rise of modern science has produced the most severe crisis for belief. Auguste Comte divided the history of human thought into three stages, the theological, the metaphysical, and finally the positivist in which man's reason will be free from the illusion of belief in God. But Comte did not anticipate the development in modern religion of a post-positivist stage. After the work of empirical criticism has exposed the errors of a simple literalism, we may be free to explore the deeper strata of meaning in the traditional symbols as fundamental expressions of the human situation which are not dissolved by the scientific picture of the world. The mystery of creation and man's sense of relationship to a divine creative power remain when the details of creation stories are recognized as myths. The story of the fall of man from an original innocence and perfection expresses man's experience of estrangement from his essential being and a fulfillment for which he longs, and yet which he cannot grasp. The discovery of a mercy and renewal which come from beyond man himself comes as a genuine experience of the divine power, although traditional expressions of its working, whether in the Buddhist doctrine of the Bodhisattvas, or the Christian doctrines of atonement, may be understood as symbolic expressions of truths about the ultimate realities of personal existence and history.

Even if we conclude that these symbols offer a legitimate way of preserving religious truth, we should not underestimate the intellectual struggle which is required to achieve an authentic expression of religious faith consonant with twentieth century science and the new cosmologies. In the Christian tradition the controversy over Rudolph Bultmann's interpretation of the Christian scripture in terms of existentialist philosophy offers an example of the critical issues. Bultmann wants to reinterpret the biblical symbols of the fall, guilt, and redemption by showing how the ancient forms gave expression to man's existential questions and his self-interpretation. Bultmann's analysis of the existential questions is drawn largely from Heidegger's philosophy. He interprets the Christian Gospel as an answer, known only through personal faith, to the question about the meaning of existence. Bultmann is attacked on every side. There are the conservatives who do not want to disturb the ancient modes of expression. There are those who recognize the mythological elements in religion but are dubious of attempts to translate these into philosophical terms. And there are those who stand outside the Christian faith and who ask, "Why is not man's existential self-understanding enough, why should he return to an ancient faith at all?" The outcome in this struggle is not decided by intellectual analysis alone. The depths of spiritual life are involved. It is an issue concerning ultimate commitments and loyalties. It is the issue of how man is to find the meaning of his life.

What is happening in the discussion with Bultmann is happening in all the great religious traditions. In Formosa Neo-Confucians are seeking to show how the Confucian tradition can both absorb and deepen the scientific mentality through reaffirmation of the Confucian moral perspective. Japanese Buddhists are re-examining the Buddhist doctrine of desire in an effort to preserve the vital discipline of the self in relation to a life in a technological age. The Hindu philosopher Radhakrishnan proposes a synthesis of the Hindu tradition with modern idealistic philosophy as qualified and informed by Western themes and motifs.[6] As an example of the intellectual ferment we are describing we can note a report concerning the program of the Ahmadiyya movement of Islam at work in Africa, where Islam is making a strong bid for the allegiance of the emerging nations. A reporter says:

> The Ahmadiyya movement claims to do three things—to reform and purge Islam itself: to express Islam in ways pertinent to the modern world; and to answer the challenge of Christianity by borrowing from Christian faith and practise. It is now proposing to set up a medical mission in Sierra Leone, and its schools are increasing in number.[7]

Is this reinterpretation and adjustment of the religious tradition a genuine advance in man's spiritual adventure or a futile last ditch stand before the onslaught of a radical new human outlook? It depends on where one stands how he answers this question. In Western culture there are some hopeful signs that the inherited forms of faith can receive authentic contemporary expression. Some of those signs are found in the realm of religious art. Matisse's Chapelle du Rosaire in Vence, Le Corbusier's at Ronchamp, and other achievements in church architecture are such signs. Contemporary painting has given only a few examples of convincing religious expression, though many find such in Rouault. But in music the case is clearer. The great *Te Deum* and other choral works of Ralph Vaughan Williams, Benjamin Britten's *Noah,* the Masses by Stravinsky and Poulenc communicate religious meaning in a contemporary idiom. The systematic theologies of Paul Tillich and Karl Barth are reinterpretations of the traditional theological materials in ways which seek to be relevant to the present without dissipating the substance of the traditional faith, though Tillich conceives the method of reinterpretation quite differently from Barth. And it should not be forgotten that those who stand outside the historic faiths often draw directly or indirectly upon their substance. Albert Camus took the title for his book *The Fall (La Chute)* from the Christian tradition. This book and many others by him are filled with biblical themes although he rejects in part their traditional interpretation. Religious symbols do retain their power in a scientifically minded age.

2

There are many religions, and the second major issue to be considered is the attitude the religions take toward one another. There is a fundamental distinction here between such religions as Hinduism and Buddhism which in principle claim not to displace other faiths, and Judaism, Islam, and Christianity which have historically claimed a revelation of the divine which in the end must overcome all diversity of faith.

In Christianity today there is a deep self-examination on this issue, for it goes to the heart of the Christian conception of God. How does He deal with His creatures? Is Christianity the climax of a history of redemption which has its anticipations in all human experience? Or does Christianity assert, as some contemporary theologies hold, that the one revelation which created the

155

Judaeo-Christian peoples leads to the judgment that all man's religiousness outside this revelation is only a misunderstanding of God's nature and a reflection of man's self worship? Professor Toynbee sharply raises the question of what lies back of such an exclusive claim when he asks:

> Does not any creature stand convicted of megalomania if he allows himself to imagine that God can have committed Himself in an annunciation to one or more of His creatures, or, still more preposterous, in a covenant with one or more of them, at a particular point in Space-Time, to making this particular encounter of theirs with Him into the supreme moment in the history of His creation?[8]

Now the charge of megalomania is a hard one to answer. Hinduism with its proclamation of synthesis in which all religions can find shelter, and be reconciled in the Absolute One which dissolves all diversity, is attractive religiously because it offers a way of unity, and ethically because it expresses a spirit of tolerance and understanding.

But there is a danger of obscuring the real issue when the argument is put at the level of megalomania. The question is whether in our relation to the Holy we are led to some decisions as to the character of the Holy and as to the nature of the response which is required of us. One cannot believe all at once in the divine reality in all the forms which the great religions have conceived it, a point Toynbee himself makes. The Buddhist Hinayana goal of the extinction of the self's desire in order that it attain Nirvana cannot be simply reconciled with the Mahayana Buddhist view that the enlightened one may make himself responsible for the salvation of others. God cannot be the absolute spirit of Hindu advaita (non-dualist) doctrine utterly beyond all time and limitation, and at the same time be the creating, caring, responding God of history of the Christian scripture. Whoever the true God is, human culture is full of false Gods and false conceptions of God. Toynbee says that the absolutizing of our particular religious faith comes from the desire to escape the risk of making decisions, which in the end causes us to acknowledge issues between different ways of conceiving the divine.

Once we have seen, however, that the issue cannot be resolved simply by charging with intolerance those who claim a truth others do not have, we can acknowledge that there is one position which can be taken within the exclusive faiths. That is, *no existing conception of the Holy is exhaustive*. What Dr. Hocking has called *reconception* of one's own faith in the light of the meeting with new concepts and experience is always a possibility. That is why the encounter of one religious tradition with another may result in creativity for both. The meeting of the major traditions on a basis of mutual respect is surely one of the significant possibilities in our century. In many places such meeting comes in the course of life as people of differing traditions find themselves with common concerns. One thinks of Moslem business men on Y.M.C.A. boards in the Near East, of Hindus engaged in the discussion of modern philosophy with Western Christians, of humanists and Neo-Confucianists teaching in Christian colleges, and of the wide general interest in the study of history of religions. We may indeed invite disillusionment if we expect from such meeting and discussion any achievement of consensus. Is that even a desirable goal? We may treasure the richness of perspective which comes from the many religions, even if we are among those who hold that one requires a final judgment upon the others. But it requires a commitment to open search and discussion to rise above parochial prejudice. We have to acknowledge that our self interest and defensiveness are inevitably aroused in the meeting of alternative religious outlooks, so Professor Toynbee's warning is relevant.

In this new world-wide encounter the religions are on trial before one another, and before human judgment, for there ought to be that in the religious spirit which makes it possible for men to respect one another's humanity, to listen to one another's view of life, and to exhibit a spirit of charity and humility in human relationships. Can the sorry story of religious hatred be overcome? Can men preserve, treasure and renew their religious loyalties in a spirit of human brotherliness? It is always discouraging to see religious people quarreling over who it is that understands love most fully. The threat of "syncretism" should not be allowed to prevent us from recognizing that a real mutual encounter and influence is inevitable and salutary in the world today. Religion should not be a source of the deepening of the chasms between men. They are deep enough as it is.

Such an encounter of religions presupposes freedom for the encounter, and this means we must here take notice of the issue of the place of the religious community in the state, though in the scope of this paper, we can only mention the complex problems. Persecution both against religion and in the name of religion exists in the twentieth century as it has in every previous one. The religious community which seeks to worship a reality which stands above the state or nation may find itself suspect, and under repression, if not outright persecution. Freedom of worship is still one of the threatened goods of a mature civilization.

Religious communities generally are concerned with more than freedom for their thought and worship. They are concerned with the life of the community and with their contribution to both the support and the criticism of the common life. Most of the religion in the world's history has existed in some kind of social or political establishment. There are many types of establishment today, and many movements toward a more explicit place for the religious community in the natural life. Thailand is a Buddhist state, Islam is the state religion of Pakistan and Malaya. There is the Roman Catholic establishment in Spain, and the Anglican establishment in England. There are strong movements in Burma and Ceylon toward a more explicit established status of Buddhism. These examples can be contrasted with that of the United States where the religious institutions have no establishment. The issues in this case have to do with the areas of remaining privilege, the relationship of state support to religious schools, and with moral issues where the influence of the religious community makes itself felt on questions of state policy.

The forms of the relationship of religious communities to the societies in which they live are varied and complex. No general and clear trend in our time is discernible. Issues concerning religious institutions will continue to be raised in every political community, and many factors of tradition, national ideals, and conceptions of freedom will affect national policies. Every concordat between a religious institution and the state is certain to be an uneasy one in a world where the forces of political life are so explosive. There are many cross-currents of feeling and judgment on this issue within the religious communities themselves. In Malaya there is a law which requires every Moslem to attend the mosque on Fridays, and the religious courts can assess a twenty-five dollar fine for failure to comply. During the summer of 1960 a Malayan official, a Moslem, made a public plea that the courts not enforce this law because of the appearance it would give Malaya in the eyes of other freedom loving countries. Thus nationalistic, democratic and religious motives are intertwined in public policy. Religious groups vary as to the kind of political status they seek. Some are concerned only to secure freedom for worship and beyond that point have no direct interest in the forms of political life. Others hold that the religious community must find ways to bring its inspiration and influence into the common life while retaining the ultimate perspective, and critical judgment without which human affairs tend to lose their true direction.

3

So far we have been asking about those issues which arise within the religious traditions today. There is an alternative position. Many religious people believe that the integrity and vitality of the religious spirit require in our time that it be set free from just those involvements with tradition, those efforts to adjust ancient concepts to present realities which engage the energies of the traditionalists. They hold that a change in religious concepts as radical as that brought about by the modern scientific conception of nature is required, and they believe that the religious spirit can be relevant in our century only as it goes all the way toward adoption of a scientific and rational method of approaching religious truth.

These are the ones who "cannot go home again" to any of the traditions. They see the religious traditions as having been formed in the primitive and adolescent phases of human evolution, and they seek a new and "mature" religious faith. The psychologist Henry A. Murray writes of the need for a "mythology for grown ups" which will preserve the riches of religious tradition, but will bring new insight from new levels of human understanding. Professor Goodenough has entitled his book on religion, *Toward a Mature Faith.*[9]

I shall call those who take this position the New Deists because they have a close kinship with the eighteenth century deists in basic outlook, though this is a *new* deism, based on a new era of scientific thought. The early deists wanted a rational religion free from the encumbrance of outworn belief. They wanted a religious outlook agreeable with and indeed based upon the scientific view of the world which had achieved its greatest triumph in Newton's physics. They believed that Newtonian science supported rational arguments for God, freedom, and immortality. Earlier deism had an ethical concern, and tended to become primarily an ethical faith. Believing that reason unites where tradition divides, the deists sought universal rational moral principles which they believed were legislated and enforced by the Supreme Being as laws of his universe. They upheld religions as the inspiration of virtuous conduct and the encouragement of belief in a heavenly reward.

Most of these themes reappear in the New Deism of the twentieth century. To mention representative figures, there are Julian Huxley, Lewis Mumford, Edmund Sinnott, Erwin Goodenough, Norman Cousins, and Pierre de Chardin, the last a Roman Catholic who explored many themes in the relation of an evolutionary world-view to religious faith. Some aspects of the New Deism are derived from the advances in science since the eighteenth century. Physics has undergone a revolution in basic concepts, and leaves far more open questions than did Newton's science. With Darwin the evolutionary perspective has entered, and the new deism is especially concerned with a dynamic view of the universe. In psychology the new deism is more complex and sophisticated than was the simple associationist psychology of the eighteenth century. Freudianism and the depth psychology movement have stressed the irrational elements in human nature. And no contemporary view of man can help but be sobered and perplexed by the outburst of demonic passion and cruelty in the concentration camps and other exhibitions of twentieth century man's ruthlessness to man.

With these qualifications however, it can still be said that what is characteristic of the New Deism as of the old is its temper of scientific rigor, its belief in moral sanity through rational control, its optimism about man's possibilities and its sense of man's at-homeness in the universe, its preservation of belief in God while it remains highly critical of traditional concepts of God. It is a positive, aggressive, morally sensitive and committed outlook, seeking a faith integrated with contemporary modes of thought. Norman Cousins has put into his *Litany for Modern Man* an articulation of this basic faith. I shall not quote all of it, but hope that these lines convey the sense of the whole:

> I am a single cell in a body of two billion cells. The body is mankind.
> I glory in the individuality of self, but my individuality does not separate me from my universal self—the oneness of man.
>
>   ✳   ✳   ✳
>
> I do not believe that human kind is an excrescence or a machine, or that the myriads of solar systems and galaxies in the universe lack order or sanction.
> I may not embrace or command this universal order, but I can be at one with it for I am of it.
>
>   ✳   ✳   ✳
>
> I see no separation between the universal order and the moral order.
>
>   ✳   ✳   ✳
>
> The sense of human unity makes possible a *reverence for life*.
>
>   ✳   ✳   ✳
>
> I will work for human unity under a purposeful peace. I will work for the growth of a moral order that is in keeping with the universal order.
> In this way do I affirm faith in life and life in faith.
> I am a single cell in a body of two billion cells. The body is mankind.[10]

Here rationalism is joined with mystical religious feeling in a way which is not always present in deism, but the central theme of confidence in the unity of man with his world and of man with man through rational insight is the key to the position.

When Norman Cousins here speaks of "reverence for life," he brings us deliberately to the figure of Albert Schweitzer, one of the few persons in the world who cannot be omitted in any study of the religious situation in our time. He cannot be classified among the "new deists" for he does not belong with them philosophically or theologically. His roots are in the Christian faith, and in the spirit of the enlightenment, and he combines these in a way which is peculiar to him, so that he stands apart. In his principle of "reverence for life" he accepts the positive Christian evaluation of life with its doctrine of the goodness of the creation, yet he seems to develop this as a principle which transcends any particular tradition. And in his example of devotion, of moral dedication and the will to reconciliation his spiritual stature makes him the symbol and inspiration of the sacrificial spirit which has commanded the response of sensitive souls throughout the world. It is characteristic of those I have called the New Deists that often they find in Albert Schweitzer a major source of inspiration and insight.

But Schweitzer's complex ethical and religious outlook is at many points at variance with the view that a rationally unified whole can be made out of science and human experience. Schweitzer sees as Thomas Hardy did, an ultimate opposition between the demands of a humane ethic and the ways of nature. Schweitzer says:

> . . . ethics can expect nothing from a true knowledge of the world . . . The world offers us the disconcerting spectacle of the will to life in conflict with itself. One existence maintains itself at the expense of another.[11]

This thesis directly challenges the deistic confidence that the natural order and the moral order exhibit mutual support. Late in 1960 a group of Schweitzer's American followers made a pilgrimage to Lambarene with the specific purpose of asking him about this radical opposition between ethics and nature.[12]

There are two major issues which the new deism faces. The first concerns the extent to which religious faith can find its principles and its rational ground in the objective inspection of the conditions of human life in nature. Deists reject the authority of special revelations or special intuitions of the divine. They want to find a position which in principle is accessible to all rational men, precisely in order to set religion free from the bias, the defensiveness, and the confusion which result from appeal to authorities beyond the reach of criticism. The question arises then as to how religious knowledge is to be derived from experience.

Dr. W. F. G. Swann, director for thirty-two years of the Bartol Research Foundation in Philadelphia, and one of the elder statesmen of modern physical science, writes in a religious vein of the mystery and miraculous character of all nature and life. He raises, in fashion reminiscent of that earlier deist William Paley, the question of whether the universe exhibits a "planned design, whether or not we are willing to admit the notion of a planner, or say what we mean by that postulate?" Then he comments on how we are to deal with such questions:

> In discussing such matters I think it is essential to avoid all theological doctrine as a starting point. I would rather see a theological doctrine emerge spontaneously as part of the over-all scheme of nature, than I would see the workings of nature forced into a frame provided by a preconceived theological doctrine as a starting point.[13]

The thesis of both old and new deism could not be put more succinctly. We are to see the truth of the divine reality by freeing ourselves from the bias of inherited theology, and discovering the truth which rises "spontaneously" from the general scheme of nature.

But what truth rises spontaneously from the face of nature? For Thomas Hardy it was the truth of a relentless machine grinding its way forward. For Bertrand Russell it is the trampling march of unconscious power. For Albert Schweitzer it is the contradiction between the struggle for life and the demands of conscience. Are the issues here resolved by further appeal to the observable facts, or do they lead us into the area of evaluation rooted in the perspectives of different faiths, with their different responses to the facts?

If we read the facts differently, and interpret their implications differently, this must be partly because we seek the meaning of life as different selves, shaped by historical traditions, with different perspectives and different ultimate commitments. How can these differences be adjudicated and by what higher judgments can they be resolved?

At this point even physics raises some questions for rationalists, since the relativity of the perspective in which we see the facts is now a factor in physical theory. And when we make judgments in history we recognize the clash of ultimate values. The issue here concerns the ultimate ground of faith. Is there something which lies deeper than rational thought, because it grasps a reality which can only be known through the total response of the person? Or is it the case that a higher synthesis of religious experience and scientific insight, a reconciliation of intuition and reason, is possible in a more ordered and inclusive view of our life in its cosmic setting? The new deism, I suggest, lives more by the hope of such a synthesis than by its possession, but it may point toward the synthesis which must ever lure those who believe in the unity of truth.

The second issue for the new deism is related to the first. It concerns the view which is to be taken of man's potentialities for good and for evil. Two philosophies of man are in contention in our day. One is that which sees in man an essential goodness, and a creative capacity. He can find the resources within himself to meet the experiences of life and the fate of death with courage and be at peace with them. The other sees a contradiction in man's spirit which he cannot resolve by his own efforts. His existence involves a final anxiety about his being, about the world, and life. He is therefore prone to take desperate measures to assure himself of his security, either in pride or in despairing resignation. The religions have expressed both these attitudes and have ministered to both of them.

The issues here, it may be fairly clear, cannot be resolved solely by an appeal to common knowledge. Every religious outlook will have to come to terms with both human hopefulness and with human desperation. The twentieth century has shown the highest technical achievements in human history. It is also the century of Auschwitz and countless other examples of man's cruelty to man. No theology or religion which does not recognize both sides of man's nature can claim the thoughtful allegiance of twentieth century minds. Here we have raised an issue which helps us see the relevance of the religious traditions with their symbols of man's estrangement from God, and their declaration of the necessity of repentance and regeneration. A superficial rational optimism can be just as completely out of touch with the realities of human experiences as is sentimentalized religious faith. It remains to be seen how far a rational humanism can clarify, purge, and fulfill man's highest capacities without the religious awareness of the divine holiness, judgment, and mercy.

I am trying only to state an issue not to resolve it; but we may have gone far enough in the analysis to see that traditionalists and modernists, mystics and rationalists, and surely those who have high hopes for man and those who see tragic elements in his destiny may speak in the twentieth century with insight, power, and relevance. None has a monopoly on the truth.

The ultimate issue in religion in our century and in every century concerns the meaning of man's life and the question about God as the source and fulfillment of the meaning of all existence. As Alfred North Whitehead has said, "To-day there is but one religious dogma in debate: What do you mean by 'God'?"[14] Is man the creature of a divine reality which gives meaning and fulfillment to his struggles, or is man, alone in the cosmos, required to set his own spirit free, bear his own burdens and become a saint without God as Albert Camus describes man's situation in his novel *The Plague*. We ask this question, not because we have inherited something called religious belief, but because we are men who live and love and die. *In Science and the Modern World* Whitehead states the meaning of religion in these words:

> Religion is the vision of something which stands beyond, behind, and within, the passing flux of immediate things; something which is real, and yet waiting to be realised; something which is a remote possibility, and yet the greatest of present facts; something that gives meaning to all that passes, and yet eludes apprehension; something whose possession is the final good, and yet is beyond all reach; something which is the ultimate ideal, and the hopeless quest....
>
> Apart from it, human life is a flash of occasional enjoyments lighting up a mass of pain and misery, a bagatelle of transient experience.[15]

It may obscure the real issue even to use the word God for that which Whitehead speaks about here, since we have no right to say that only one kind of language is appropriate for that which stands beyond all language. Dr. Tillich has used the phrase "the God beyond God" to remind us that we are speaking about One who cannot be confined to our human perspectives. If God be God, the One who can save life from ultimate chaos, He is not a projection of a father image, or a symbol for our best human ideals. He is the reality which judges all our ideals. As Henry Nelson Wieman has said, "God is more than we can think."[16] He is the truth of all truths, the source of being, the spirit which makes us persons, able to approach Him in thought and worship.

Is such a God real? That is the religious issue in every century, as Thomas Hardy saw. He could not let go of the question. In the closing passage of *The Dynasts* he has the Spirit of the Pities ask if after all the Great Impersonal Source may not be conscious life since it has produced conscious human life, and Hardy allows the Spirits to echo the *Magnificat,* "thou hast put down the mighty [the Dynasts] from their seats."

Can man in this technological age with its high possibilities of creativity and its terrifying possibilities of destruction live with a faith and a hope which will release his full humanity, his capacity to love and to serve in the midst of human problems? That is the religious question to which men of the twentieth century must give such answers as they have.

Notes

1. Quoted in W. R. Rutland, *Thomas Hardy, A Study of His Writings and their Background,* Oxford, Blackwell (1938), p. 64.
2. Reported in the London *Observer,* October 16, 1960.
3. Friedrich Nietzsche, *Thus Spake Zarathustra,* LXVI.

4. Martin Buber, *I and Thou,* Eng. trans. by Ronald Gregor Smith, Edinburgh, 1937.
5. Boris Pasternak, *Doctor Zhivago,* Pantheon Books edition, N.Y., 1958, p. 49.
6. S. Radhakrishnan, *East and West, Some Reflections,* London, Allen & Unwin, 1955.
7. Cecil Northcott in *The Scotsman,* Edinburgh, December 5, 1960.
8. Arnold Toynbee, *An Historian's Approach to Religion,* London, Oxford University Press, 1956, p. 135.
9. Henry A. Murray, "A Mythology for Grownups," *The Saturday Review,* January 23, 1960, pp. 8–12.
   Erwin Goodenough, *Toward a Mature Faith,* New York, Prentice Hall, 1955.
10. Norman Cousins, "Litany for Modern Man," *The Saturday Review,* Aug. 8, 1953, p. 22. (Italics the present writer's.)
11. Albert Schweitzer, "The Problem of Ethics for Twentieth Century Man," *The Saturday Review,* June 13, 1953, p. 48.
12. Reported in the *London Times,* December 29, 1960.
13. W.F.G. Swann, "The Living and the Dead," *The Saturday Review,* June 4, 1960, p. 44.
14. A. N. Whitehead, *Religion in the Making,* New York, Macmillan, 1926, p. 67.
15. A. N. Whitehead, *Science and the Modern World,* New York, Macmillan, 1931, p. 275.
16. Henry N. Wieman, "God is More Than We Can Think," *Christendom,* Vol. I (1935–6) pp. 428, 442.

Literary Possibilities of the Next Decade

Richard W. B. Lewis

NOTHING IS MORE DANGEROUS THAN TO MAKE PREDICTIONS ABOUT the future of literature; and yet to do so has been a kind of mania in every American generation. The literary act—unlike the political act, for example, or the scientific inquiry—is essentially unplanned. It can even be said to be involuntary: the result, that is, not of any thrust of the will, but rather of a chance firing of the creative imagination as it responds to largely unpredictable proddings from within and without. Writers in America, moreover (the best of them anyhow), have normally been loath to huddle together in labelled groups and to announce a common intention in those manifestoes that are a regular sign of new developments in Europe. Guesses of the sort I have been invited to offer are therefore vulnerable to swift and derisive repudiation; but it can be remembered, at least, that Americans have always had a peculiar relish for offering—and accepting—such invitations, for speculating as to which way the imagination will jump in this country, and indeed as to what might come next in all other human activities as well.

Ralph Waldo Emerson, himself the most seismographically

171

accurate trend-spotter America has known, was wittily scornful of the practice he did much to establish. He referred to an elderly gentleman of his acquaintance who insisted on his after-dinner nap being interrupted every ten minutes so that he might be told the latest news. We are always asking what's new, Emerson said, as though the old were so bad. More recently and more relevantly, the extravagantly gifted poet Hart Crane (who died in 1932), put the case with a shrewd vehemence. "I think," Crane wrote to a friend, "that this unmitigated concern with the future is one of the most discouraging symptoms of the chaos of our age. ... It seems as though the imagination had ceased all attempts at any creative activity, and has become simply a great bulging eye ogling the foetus of the next century." Even if, more modestly, we ogle only the foetus of the next decade, we may be exposing ourselves to a similar disheartening diagnosis.

The lust for prophesying about literature, and about everything else, has been more marked of late than usual: partly, I suppose, because it is handy to think in terms of decades, and we are at the start of a new one; and partly, no doubt, because we seem to be entering into a new political climate that could conceivably affect the weather throughout the whole of life. Our men of letters were right to rejoice, albeit with an air of staring unbelief, when our political representative invited a great poet to read one of his finest poems at the recent inaugural proceedings; and when, during a subsequent television program devoted to Robert Frost, the President appeared to speak of Frost in language startlingly free of the heavy and ignorant clichés customarily used by public men in talking about poets, and in fact with an expert emphasis not on Frost's homespun geniality but on his skepticism, his sense of darkness, his sturdy awareness of human limits. However, the relationship between literary activity and the political element—between art and the political order—is a fascinat-

172

ingly complex affair that I want to investigate a little later. And
in any case, it is probably better to begin with the gloomier phases
of our situation and the possibilities it holds, and then to search
for some grounds of hope. So let me suggest that the current in-
tensive guessing about our literary future reflects a good deal of
the condition deplored by Hart Crane. It reflects a feeling that the
age we actually inhabit is too chaotic for the imagination to take
hold of, and that the best the imagination can do is to peer into
a future that might be more hospitable to the creative impulse.

Amid the jumble of our history, the violently conflicting demands on our allegiances, the lightning mutations of so much
that we observe and the sheer unreality of so much that we
experience, where can the imagination find a subject that will
stand still long enough to be caught and represented by the
resources of art? The state of the theater in America today is a
bleakly revealing point to depart from; for the state of the
theater is that, in any serious sense, it does not at the moment
happen to exist, and for very telling reasons. I do not mean, of
course, that plays, or rather "shows," are not being spasmodically
produced, nor that they are without exception boring; certainly
I am not implying a cultural need for plays with more misery in
them, and less comedy, though perhaps one could make do with
fewer papier-maché Orientals. It is only that the works produced
and performed these days do not compose anything one could
reasonably call a theater; nor is it possible that they should.

The theater as such is an institution that flourishes at the center
of a culture. That center may be located in the annual rites and
festivals of a community religion, as in the age of Pericles; or
amid the purposive energies of a burgeoning national and urban
life, as in Elizabethan London; or in the narrower circles of
court and nobility, as in seventeenth century France. But only
under circumstances like those can the theater—by mirroring in

manifold perspective the existent and accessible cultural center—perform its true and traditional function: namely, of showing the very age and body of the time its form and pressure. America since the second war has not been able to exhibit any such center—as it could, for instance, in the vigorous movements of social and implicitly of moral reform that emanated out of Washington in the Rooseveltian thirties, when we were being enjoined to "think along *national* lines." But today the dramatic talent, lacking any discernible center by which and through which it can mirror aspects of the whole body of our time, withers away in the concocting of ephemeral shows; or is driven to addressing the peripheries of life and what is significantly called "*off*-Broadway"; or it has fallen to writing articles in the *Times* about the future of the theater. That future is altogether sure; for it is co-existent with the future of American society and culture; and only if the latter recover their fiber and manifest again some meaningful momentum, spiritual and practical energies flowing forth like radii from the center of a circle, will the theater in America come back to life.

There is evidence that some of our younger contemporary novelists see themselves in a comparable dilemma; and that they, too, find their world bereft of shape and deficient in artistically manageable reality. According to one sympathetic commentator, novelists have been seized with a "deeply lodged suspicion" not merely that the age is turbulent without being sensible, and uproarious without being real; but "that the power to alter the course of the age . . . is actually vested nowhere." Quoting that remark, Philip Roth, the National Book Award winner in fiction for 1959, is quick to acknowledge that the responsibility for such a suspicion may not lie outside the writer at all, but may be "nothing more than the absence of genius in our time." Even so, he is compelled to add what he regards as troubling news: that writers of fiction in our time have suffered nothing less than a loss of subject. "The community," says Mr. Roth, "is, properly, both [the writer's] subject and his audience." But a community —that is, a culture with a detectable heart rhythmically animating it—is just what we seem not to belong to, or to comprise. Until or unless a community rises into being in America, under whatever political or moral or religious pressures, fiction would appear to be as ill-fated as drama. As a matter of fact, American fiction since the second war has come up with the most promising and courageous of the responses to the cultural predicament it has been the first to emphasize. The response of post-war fiction, indeed, has involved a cunning exploitation of that very predicament. To grasp the extent of its accomplishment (and this, ultimately, will be the chief hopeful burden of my remarks), we ought to enlarge our context by taking some soundings in poetry and criticism.

One feels more dubious about trying to discern the present and immediate future of poetry than of any other realm of literature. It is already apparent, perhaps, that the present generation is not blessed with the remarkable distinction of its predecessor. It cannot show a galaxy of poetic talent to match the one composed of Wallace Stevens and Hart Crane, of T. S. Eliot and Robert Frost, of Ezra Pound, E. E. Cummings, William Carlos Williams, and Marianne Moore. Those are the names we associate with the creative explosion of the twenties, what the critic R. P. Blackmur has called the *anni mirabiles* of the artistic imagination, the last stupendous age of literature not only in poetry but in fiction and the other arts, and not only in America but equally in England and Ireland and France and Germany as well; it is improbable that this century will look upon its like again. But if it is impossible to discover in post-war poetry names of such a high and richly varied order, it is also impossible not

175

to recognize that more poetry is being written here today and more poetry of an unmistakably competent, a deeply and durably disciplined kind than there was in the previous generation or in any previous generation in American history.

In poetry, the possibilities are, quantitatively speaking, excellent; but beyond the quantitative remark, one does not proceed with much assurance. For one thing, the poetry in question is almost exclusively lyric poetry; and lyric poetry is more concerned than are fiction and drama with the strange privacies of individual experience and perception; and it is far more bound up with its own formalities and technicalities. The future of lyric poetry is more likely to depend on shifts in the fashions of metrics than shifts in the winds of doctrine. One can, however, attempt a few trial notations and get at some of the other edges of the situation. And one of the facts worth noticing is that, partly because of the continuing primacy of technique and of the personal or idiosyncratic in American poetry, post-war literary criticism has moved its attention away somewhat from poetry and towards fiction. The earlier generation of critics was largely occupied with the art of poetry, with the magical and hidden powers of words, with the delicate structures of metaphor, with paradox and irony and the rest. Most of those critics were themselves practicing poets of greater or lesser ability: Eliot and Pound, of course, but also writers like R. P. Blackmur, Allen Tate, Robert Penn Warren, John Crowe Ransom and Kenneth Burke. It is a brilliant and distinguished group. The service it has rendered the world of letters in America is incalculable; for it served to cultivate the American sensibility, and the uncultivated sensibility is no less dismal and dangerous than the unillumined heart. Its influence, happily, is still strong and salutary. And yet the criticism that has made its mark since the war has tended to be interested in literature that engages thicker and more palpable chunks of life than lyric poetry has normally been able to do; or at least than most of the poetry that stimulated the criticism of the pre-war years.

When the younger critics talk about poetry, they are likely to talk not about the structures of the lyric but about the range of longer and more comprehensive poems—about *The Faerie Queene* or *Don Juan* or Whitman's "Song of Myself" or Hart Crane's symbolist epic *The Bridge*. They are more likely still to discuss the art of the novel, and to discuss it in a broad context of history and sociology, of politics and morality and psychology, even, betimes, of metaphysics. Just as the earlier critics were often poets, so the post-war critics are at least sometimes novelists, and evince a lively interest in political entanglements and social change. Irving Howe, who writes forcibly about Faulkner and Sherwood Anderson and the European political novel, has also composed a history of the American Communist Party. Leslie Fiedler, an impish and provocative observer of fiction in many countries, also meditates the relation between American intellectuals and the late Senator McCarthy, and has a volume of short stories and a novel ready for the press. Richard Chase, a searching analyst of fiction in America, has given us a lengthy political dialogue bearing a title borrowed from Whitman, *Democratic Vistas*. And so on. If poetry before the war led criticism, so to speak, into a necessary withdrawal from history in order to attempt a crucial refinement of taste, so the post-war novel has lured criticism back into the thickets of time, and the more public arenas of experience. The distinguished French essayist, Julien Benda, would call this development, as he once called a comparable turn in his own country, a distinct intellectual betrayal; there are always those who—and not entirely without reason—foresee the ruin of art through contamination by the impurities of the actual. The risk is a real one. But America, it will

177

be remembered, has until late been unaccustomed to history; now the national consciousness is everywhere invaded by it. It would be more disturbing yet if so vital a change were not reflected among our men of letters.

Meanwhile, of course, poetry itself has not been without its own devoted and skillful commentators, any more than it has been without its gifted practitioners. Of the latter, as I have suggested, the abundance and diversity are too great to undertake a listing of even the outstanding names; should I do so, I should at once be confronted with the names of twenty more of whom I had not heard until this instant. But I think we may expect American lyric poetry in the coming years to become somewhat less lordly, less detached from the daily urgencies that beset the rest of us, less intellectual and less given to dialectical somersaults than was much of the neo-modernist poetry written by the followers of Pound and Eliot. A certain attractive roughness has been apparent in recent poetry, as though the metrics had suffered a valuable bout with reality. And although the prevailing tone continues to echo a grave awareness of the contradictions in life, a comic note has begun to creep pleasingly in. It expresses, in most cases, a sort of smiling toughness of mind on the part of those poets who, like some of the novelists, have decided that the muddle of our age had ruled out the very possibility of tragedy and had simply become ridiculous, and nowhere more so than in the effort of poetry to engage it.

The most boisterously comic poetry since the war has, needless to say, come from those artistic left-wingers known as the "beat" writers, whose work also exhibits the ripest sociological content on the contemporary literary scene. The *literature* of the beat movement is evidently not going to amount to very much; for the beat reaction has not galvanized any great degree of creative talent, while its view of the creative act is too slovenly and unde-

178

manding—guitars and *espresso* are not adequate replacements for the prolonged and painful struggle with the work-sheets. The movement in general may well continue to erupt from time to time in other and non-literary ways. To pursue that possibility would be to digress from the topic assigned; but this much should be said as relevant to certain tendencies that do concern us— namely, that the beat movement at its most authentic represents an emotional and indeed a non-sectarian religious uprising against a materialistic society and a mechanized culture bent (or so it frequently seems) on sealing up that dimension of human nature where intuition, imagination and the genuine religious sentiment have their place. Such an uprising has its historic antecedents running back through the transcendentalism of the nineteenth century and the Great (Religious) Awakening of the eighteenth century to the outburst of fevered heresies that shook the foundations of an oppressive ecclesiasticism in the late middle ages. It has its roots in the psychic structure of man; and it springs from that non-rational aspect which it is death for any culture to try to hide.

But on the more purely literary side, the beat movement has by no means been without significance. For one thing, it has offered the strenuous example of poetry that declares its remoteness from history, that noisily signs off from contemporary society, by launching savagely comic attacks on it. The most self-assertive nay-sayers to our time, the beat writers have also been the most maliciously and rambunctiously and, on occasion, even the most boldly and movingly concerned with it. For another thing (and this is really a corollary of the first), beat writing reveals to striking effect the presence within it of the two most important influences on what might be the one major development in American poetry of this decade. These two influences or ancestors —the grandfather and the father, let us say, of a truly new poetry, if we are to have one—are Walt Whitman and Hart Crane. And if their presence is, as I think, so profoundly suggestive it is because both Whitman and Crane, while masters of the lyric, of the poetry of private and inward perception, are also the two signal instances in American literary history of the poetry of epic intention.

"For my country's sake," Robert Frost said a few years ago, commenting on a number of young poets, "I might wish one or two of them an old age of epic writing. A good epic," he added with a deceptively casual air of afterthought, "would grace our history." And Frost went on in the same tone to attribute to the nineteenth century English poet, Walter Savage Landor, exactly what I would claim for Whitman and Crane. "Landor," said Frost, "has set an example in prolonging the lyric out of all bounds." That is the precise accomplishment of Crane and Whitman; they too set the example we deeply need—Whitman in "Song of Myself" and Hart Crane in *The Bridge*—in prolonging the lyric out of all bounds, expanding on that traditionally brief, sharply focussed and personal mode to the point where they could embrace, or attempt to embrace, the large perplexities of an entire culture, a whole range of history, a complete society. And that is just what the modern poet, or for that matter the modern novelist, must do if he is daring and quixotic enough to take on the epic endeavor. For the circumstantial chaos of our time—when it has not driven the writer to future-gazing or lamentation or madness—has driven him back into the confines of his private particular self as the only dependable source of usable experience. The writer cannot help but begin in the personal, that is to say in the lyric vein; the way to the more comprehensive enterprise necessarily requires a prolonging of that vein to the moment when its bounds are altogether escaped, and the self melts outward into the world.

The reason one hopes, with Frost, that such an effort does exist among the possibilities of the day is that, as Frost himself puts it, "a good epic would grace our history." It would do more; in a manner of speaking, it would help to create our history, to give it a shape and an inspiriting significance. The great example of an epic which did so is the *Aeneid* of Virgil, a poem that discovered and articulated the form potential in the long tumult of Roman history, that established the very *romanitas* of Roman culture. It was that kind of achievement that Walt Whitman had in mind when, surveying literary possibilities in the sixties of a century ago, he contended that "All else in the contributions of a nation or age, through its politics, materials, heroic personalities, military *éclat* etc., remains crude, and defers, in any close and thoroughgoing estimate, until vitalised by national, original archetypes in literature." By national, original archetypes, Whitman meant pretty much what we mean here by "epic," or at least the epic of the sort that aims at giving grace and shape to our history. And Whitman felt the need of that gift so strongly that he was willing to argue that "they only put the nation in form, finally tell anything—prove, complete anything—perpetuate anything." Those of us who feel this nation to be lacking in any form commensurate with its vigor, and our history lacking in any grace commensurate with its intensity, are therefore gratified to the point of excitement by the visible and audible presence in recent poetry of Walt Whitman and Hart Crane.

But our excitement has to be severely tempered. And it is, finally, in fiction that both our hope and our anxiety find their most logical basis. The realm of fiction, it is true, is more agitated by a sense of widespread restlessness than are the other literary realms; more charged by a conviction of old forms exhausted and new forms ready to leap into being. It palpitates more with grandeur of ambition, but for that very reason it suffers more violently from frustration. Here the felt restriction to writing with assurance only about the private self in a helpless abandonment of the rest of life is a good deal more painful. Speaking of the cultural predicament that, to his view, the writer faces today (that is, the loss of community as subject for fiction), Philip Roth concludes as follows:

> It may be that when the predicament produces in the writer not only feelings of disgust, rage and melancholy, but impotence, he is apt to lose heart, and finally . . . to turn to other matters or to other worlds; or to the self, which may, in a variety of ways, become his subject, or even the impulse of his technique. . . . The sheer fact of self, the vision of self as inviolable, powerful, and nervy, self as the only real thing in an unreal environment . . . has given to some writers joy, solace and muscle. . . . However, when the self can only be celebrated as it is excluded from society, or as it is exercised and admired in a fantastic one, we then, I think, do not have much reason to be cheery.

Coming from so talented, promising and un-histrionic a writer as Philip Roth, those advices are, indeed, anything but cheery; even if we recognize joylessly that they could have been offered in almost any earlier generation. Novelists from Cooper and Hawthorne and Melville onwards have been regularly inspired by feelings of disgust, rage and melancholy over the society they had tried to depict in fiction. They have regularly turned to other matters: to a job as inspector of customs, like Melville, or a swank and sterile position on a fashionable magazine, like Theodore Dreiser during his "ten years in the desert." They have periodically turned away from the unmanageable present world to other worlds: to the South Seas or early New England or the Venice of Cooper's *The Bravo* or the London and Paris and Rome of

Henry James or the Spain of Hemingway. Nor have they failed before our own time to locate and then to exercise the self amidst the setting of a fantastic world: Mark Twain put himself back into a comical fantasy of Arthurian England, as Hank Morgan, the Connecticut Yankee, many decades before Saul Bellow removed himself, as Henderson, the Rain King, to the tinselly wilds of a wholly artificial Africa. To recall all that is not, however, to cheer ourselves up, especially since the predicament today is without doubt considerably less bearable than it was in those other decades. But just because it is so, the achievement of American fiction since the second war is peculiarly admirable—for that achievement serves to illustrate Mr. Roth's argument in such a way, paradoxically, as in good part to undermine it.

There really is, to begin with, something we can point to as postwar fiction: a body of narrative prose that can be distinguished without difficulty from the work of Faulkner and Hemingway and Fitzgerald and their contemporaries; the work of a generation, in fact, that draws its native sustenance less from those immediate predecessors than from the great fictional giants of the nineteenth century, and especially from Melville and Mark Twain; just as the newer poetry draws less upon Eliot than upon Whitman. The names I make out for honor in the post-war generation include those of Ralph Ellison, Saul Bellow, James Purdy, William Styron, Norman Mailer, and J. D. Salinger; with others still younger coming emphatically into view. And while no single generalization could possibly hold for so varied an assortment of writers, with such critical differences of race and background and experience and temperament, it remains true that if one subject rather than another appeals strongly to most of them, it is precisely the subject of the self—of acquiring a clear sense of the self, or of hanging on against fearful odds to an integral self already in being.

It could scarcely be otherwise, and for a reason Mr. Roth has tended to skirt. For the moral and even metaphysical chaos he correctly assigns to our age is only one of its two major qualities; the other quality is a mode of response to chaos. Never was there an age that so bullied one with the pressure to conform, that grabbed at one so, that regarded the impulse to be different or simply to be left alone for a while with such grave suspicion. It is a moment when, in the compressed phrasing of E. E. Cummings, Americans appear to think

> Difference a disease of same,
> Conform the pinnacle of am.

And the current conformity—in conduct, in loyalty, in belief, in taste—is not only ferocious, a very active and militant affair; it is also the inevitable reaction of the empty-hearted to the sensation of chaos. For the kind of swirling cultural confusion we have had to experience produces conformity, and is in turn nourished and perpetuated by it. When a culture has no center to it, when there are no effectively living systems of value—religious or humanistic—by which a majority of men can conduct their lives and order and appraise their natures, then the undaring have only one recourse: to act and think and to insist others act and think like everyone else. That is a necessary Irishism, I am aware, but the situation can only be described in the kind of Irish saying that cancels itself out. Perhaps the point can be illuminated by noticing that there was really no such phenomenon as a conformist in medieval Europe or in Puritan New England; and on the contrary, that there really were heretics in those times, because there was a living orthodoxy to dissent from. Today, we do not even have heretics, for there is no total body of belief from which a man can select a fragment to commit himself to utterly:

which is the true meaning of heresy. Conformity is thus the substitute for orthodoxy in a rudderless time. It is in fact, I venture,
a version of the chaos that it responds to: a version of chaos
spuriously disguised as its opposite, as order. It is in the face of
this condition that post-war novelists have directed their imagination and their daring to resisting those terrible twins, conformity
and chaos, in a search for or an assertion of the inviolable self.

Norman Mailer—a man of disconcerting public behavior but
a writer of immense ability—gives up anything like traditional
fiction, and turns to a book that, echoing the long poem of Whitman, he calls *Advertisements for Myself;* advertisements, perhaps,
representing in our day what songs did in Whitman's. And the
theme of that curious and brilliant hodge-podge of fact and fiction
is close to the theme of Saul Bellow's novel, *The Adventures of
Augie March:* namely, a journey through a disjointed and yet
grabby world, by a person determined to be nothing but himself.
What one wise old figure says to Augie March on his travels
could be said about many of the protagonists in post-war fiction.
"All of a sudden, I catch on to something about you. You've got
opposition in you." To this young Augie agrees as though struck
by revelation: "I did have the opposition in me, and a great
desire to offer resistance and to say 'No!'" It is a desire to say No!
to all the persons and authorities and powers that, in a chaotic
time, seek to organize the spirit and to recruit and control the
man—for whatever military, political, economic, domestic, or
erotic purposes. It is a desire to fend off those elements in life to a
representative of which a character in James Purdy's less well-
known but perhaps more remarkable little novel of 1959, *Malcolm,* says: "Keep your hands off my soul." It is the same desire
that ultimately leads the nameless negro who is both narrator
and hero of Ralph Ellison's violent and comic extravaganza of
1952, *Invisible Man,* to slip away from a whole urban world

that had laid hands on his soul, and to dive down an open man-
hole in the streets of Harlem, there to take up a solitary and re-
flective underground existence.

In saying No in their very different tones of voice, these
very different selves can also be seen resisting the outward forms,
the institutional and legal forms, of contemporary life. The post-
war fictional hero is, indeed, often an outlaw of sorts, a car-
thief perhaps or an inciter of riots employed by some radical
political party. He is likely to be an object of distrust or bewilderment to the average law-abiding citizen, as the novels he in-
habits have often been the object of distrust and bewilderment
to the average law-abiding book-reviewer. But the latter only
reveals a deficient sense of metaphor. Bellow, Ellison, Purdy and
the others are not themselves criminals, nor are they advocates
of criminality. They are only indicating in their own way that
at the present moment the heroic profile cannot be created by reference to the center of the culture, for there is no center; it can
only be described negatively, in terms of what the protagonist is
able to resist or deny or escape from—as James Joyce's archetypal
modern hero, Stephen Daedalus, gained selfhood by escaping
the nets of family and church and state in his native Ireland.
The moralizing book-reviewers, moreover, reveal a deficiency in
their sense of humor. For these slippery protagonists are, to use
the old Spanish word, *picaros,* and their adventures are in the
picaresque tradition—the account of rogues on their unlawful
but primarily comical travels. The comic element is even more
central in the new fiction than it is in the new poetry; Augie
March and his colleagues represent a talent for comic scrambling
rather than a posture of romantic defiance; they resemble Charlie
Chaplin more than they do Lord Byron. Melville said about
Hawthorne (unconsciously speaking about himself) that Hawthorne said No! in thunder; but these recent picaros say no in
laughter, or while gasping for breath.

186

Still—and here I go beyond Mr. Philip Roth in my view of post-war fiction and its possibilities—the figures I have mentioned are not only comedians, outlaws, and nay-sayers; and they insist not only on the integrity of the private self. They are seekers, as well. Like the novelists who have begotten them, they are in search of a lost subject, they are hoping to discover and to enter into some lost community, to arrive at the boundaries and then at the very center of some lost order in culture and in experience. Post-war fiction, as I suggested at the outset, not only acknowledges an awareness of cultural chaos; it exploits the fact by projecting as hero a young man who makes his way through that chaos in search of a significant moral and intellectual and spiritual order with which he can meaningfully associate.

The characteristic event in the post-war novel is thus the *journey;* but it is a journey—so far—without end; which is to say that no satisfying boundaries, no stable center have yet been arrived at. For the fact is—to judge from recent fiction, anyhow—that the old subject, the old community, the old order seems past recovery. The order being sought for will require a new set of images, a new vocabulary; I even dare say, a new religious vocabulary. The old subject, the one that got lost and that was essentially Christian in definition, is no longer to be resuscitated, so the post-war novel implies. Our younger novelists evidently share the conviction of that embattled Christian apologist, the English writer C. S. Lewis, though they may not share his attitude towards the development he has announced: namely, that the modern world has become *unchristened;* so that (as Professor Lewis puts it) to the two great epochs our ancestors knew—the pre-Christian or pagan epoch, and the epoch of Christianity—we must now add a third, the one we live in, and which has to be called post-Christian.

The new American novelists, accordingly, present the engrossing dilemma of persons whose aspirations, though they are fundamentally religious in nature, cannot be fulfilled in the particular terms of the Christian religion. Those terms were available to such immediate predecessors as William Faulkner and F. Scott Fitzgerald; Faulkner could employ a phrase like "the Passion Week of the Heart," a figure of speech so highly animated by belief that it could organize and control as complex and crowded a novel as *The Sound and the Fury*. But one of the most far-reaching possibilities of the next decade is just the possibility that the fictive imagination will envisage and will dramatize for us an order of values defined in a new language, bodied forth in new metaphors. This hypothetic new structure may, of course, consist simply of new idioms for old sacraments. The old idioms, in any case, appear to have lost their vitality, or their appeal; and meanwhile the journeying heroes of post-war fiction emerge not merely as clowns but as pilgrims, too: pilgrims reverently, if haphazardly, headed for some Canterbury they think they have never known.

Perhaps we may find a clue to the possibility I mention—a new order of values, articulated in a new language—by observing the kind of order that, at its best, post-war fiction has so far been able to come up with. The most revealing instances, I fancy, are supplied by James Purdy's novel, *Malcolm,* and by Ralph Ellison's *Invisible Man*. Both instances are bright with paradox. For both Purdy and Ellison have composed a sort of inverted order—a narrative shape dragged by the vigor of art from the very shapelessness it serves to disclose; a patterned account of a world without pattern, and a world that offers no object for sustained human loyalty. *Malcolm* and *Invisible Man* are darkly comic allegories wherein the persons and situations encountered by the picaresque pilgrims are not merely random individual items; they stand for the great forces that attempt to control our lives, that badger us and smother our high intentions. Purdy's hero, an adolescent *simplicissimus,* is sought after by a series of men and women—all of them queerly stunted or off-key—who embody the lopsided contemporary power of Art, of Religion, of Money, of Erotic Love, and finally of Death. These figures lust after Malcolm's beguiling and conceivably redemptive innocence; but their effort is only to thwart the foolish fellow's effort to become fully alive. The world is constantly making him fall asleep or faint or pass out; and he finally succumbs to the death that is the truly defining force in that world. Ellison's more hectic novel is the elaboration of a basic image—that is, an image of life as a battle royal, in which young men of witless good will are required to pummel each other blind-folded, while the lords of life stand about urging the fight onwards with cynical shouts of encouragement. The hero of *Invisible Man* is catapulted through an extraordinary jumble of adventures, the clownish victim of a succession of overlords and overladies whom Ellison makes representative of the power of Race, of Education, of Technology, of Sex, and above all of Politics.

Malcolm dies and the invisible man goes underground. Their adventurous lives thus consummate themselves, and the novels they live in show a completed form. But it is an aesthetic form, designed to reveal the absence of design in the present epoch. Having said that, however, one realizes abruptly that the novel from its inception and in all countries has traditionally aimed at the very same thing; that the novel, in the words of Albert Camus, "is born simultaneously with the spirit of rebellion," and that its function is to "reject the world on account of what the world lacks." For history, human experience (now I am quoting the novelist E. M. Forster) is really "a series of *disorders,*" while art in general and the novel as its modern representative provide "the one orderly product our muddling race has produced." Have we circled laboriously through the areas of post-war literature only to conclude tamely that the new novel is like the old novel, or, Gertrude-Steinishly, that a novel is a novel and no doubt will continue to be during the next decade?

Not quite. What counts for the novelist is the extent to which the disorder he inevitably experiences gives him the stuff of creative combat; or whether it is merely something to explore and then to turn away from. Here I come back in closing, to the subject I alluded to in my beginning: the paradoxical relation between art and order, or as we now should say, between art and the perennial *dis*order of history. For one kind of disorder provides so little for a writer to rebel against that, confronting as it were an absence in reality, he can come up only with images of life ebbing away or of the individual vanishing below the surface of life. The age we have just passed through was like that, a culturally shabby moment that we shall probably refer to as the Eisenhower era, though to name it so is not to blame Mr. Eisenhower for the cultural desolation over which he presided. Our last best hope and the finest possibility of the coming years—from the literary point of view—is that, whether or not it shall be known as the Kennedy era, the age that has started will present the writer with something worth the dignity of resistance. The more vigorous and coherent the age, the more energetically the writer can honor it by his own mode of rebellion. This is why ages which have been great in other respects have also been the seed-times of great literature; not because literature announced, in those times, its complacent satisfactions with an age it was chiefly concerned to celebrate; but because the towering accomplishments of the age stirred the imagination to measure them against the still grander potentialities of the human spirit.

The writer always has a heaven in his mind; and measured against it, human life under the best of circumstances is always a mode of hell. The writer always, in the phrase of Henry James, is conscious of an order of value and beauty which this world can never show; but which this world sometimes *can* excite the imagination to envision more clearly. Mention of Henry James, however, reminds one of another remark of his, and one not less suitable to this occasion—as a caution against just such speculation and guessing as I have delayed you with. In 1889, James was invited to address a gathering at Deerfield, Massachusetts, on the future of the novel. What he said to the participants, in a letter regretting his inability to attend, is what I should say to you and more emphatically yet to myself. "Oh do something—from your point of view. An ounce of example is worth a ton of generalising." The literary possibilities of the next decade will consist not of what we guess, but of what we do.